FREELANCE WRITING FOR MAGAZINES AND NEWSPAPERS

Other books by Marcia Yudkin

MAKING GOOD: Private Business in Socialist China

GUIDEBOOK FOR PUBLISHING PHILOSOPHY
(with Janice Moulton)

FREELANCE WRITING FOR MAGAZINES AND NEWSPAPERS

Breaking In Without Selling Out

Marcia Yudkin

PERENNIAL LIBRARY

HARPER & ROW, PUBLISHERS, New York
Cambridge, Philadelphia, San Francisco
London, Mexico City, São Paulo, Singapore, Sydney

FREELANCE WRITING FOR MAGAZINES AND NEWSPAPERS. Copyright ©
1987, 1988 by Marcia Yudkin. All rights reserved. Printed in the
United States of America. No part of this book may be used or
reproduced in any manner whatsoever without written permission
except in the case of brief quotations embodied in critical articles
and reviews. For information address Harper & Row, Publishers,
Inc., 10 East 53rd Street, New York, N.Y. 10022. Published simultaneously in Canada by Fitzhenry & Whiteside Limited, Toronto.

FIRST EDITION

Designer: Ruth Bornschlegel

Library of Congress Cataloging-in-Publication Data

Yudkin, Marcia.
  Freelance writing for magazines and newspapers.

  Includes index.
  1. Authorship. 2. Feature writing. 3. Technical writing. I. Title.
PN147.Y84   1988   808'.02   88-45074
ISBN 0-06-055134-8
ISBN 0-06-273278-1 (pbk.)

For my father,
who found his own path, too

Contents

Contents

Acknowledgments

I'd like to thank the following people for useful feedback and suggestions: Nancy Hopkin, Peter Desmond, Barbara Beckwith, Florence and Gila Yudkin, members of the marketing support group of the National Writers Union, Boston local and my freelance writing students at the University of Massachusetts at Amherst.

1 / Writing as Communication

Of all the ambitious dreams, secret and otherwise, that people harbor, one of the most common is seeing one's by-line and words in print. Some would-be writers fantasize about strangers recognizing their name from books and articles. Thoughts of million-dollar book advances or expenses-paid assignments set the blood of others buzzing. Still others may see success as revenge on their junior high school English teacher or a know-it-all college roommate. These satisfactions are possible results of freelance writing, but in this book I assume that your primary motive for trying to get into print is that you have something to say and you want to communicate your tales, ideas or skills in periodicals that will reach audiences you respect.

Although this book thoroughly covers the basics of getting published, in spirit it differs from most other books on the subject. Some urge freelancers to aim only at the most lucrative or easy markets. Others show people with a vague "desire to write" how to find something—anything—to write about. Most advise writers to twist their vision to fit some standard mold. In contrast, I assume that for you, a by-line and a check aren't enough; you want to communicate with integrity. By "integrity" I mean a fine-tuned sense of responsibility to yourself, to your subject and to your audience. Rejecting the philosophy of publication at any cost sometimes complicates the options, but what's the point if the printed article provokes a rotten feeling in your gut?

I have written this book to share what I've learned about

freelancing since I published my first article for pay, in the *New York Times* education supplement, in 1981. Since then, I've had a wide variety of successes and failures. To help you avoid my mistakes, I've included many lessons I learned the hard way in my search for both income and satisfaction from communicating in print. I've come to the conclusion that combining the habits of a professional with the spirit of an amateur is the surest way to achieve publications you can be proud of.

Throughout this work I concentrate on breaking into magazines and newspapers, since few writers start off with books. While the focus here is on nonfiction, my advice in Chapters 9 through 16 applies to fiction as well.

2 / Idea to Audience

Questions, opinions, expertise, experiences and investigations that could be developed into articles are as uncountable and ephemeral as the clouds shifting around moment by moment in the atmosphere. Comparatively few ever materialize in print. Why those, and how? A successful transit from idea to audience begins with the contact between the writer and the magazine or newspaper. Either (1) the author sends the publication a query letter detailing the proposed article and explaining her or his qualifications; or (2) the author submits a completed manuscript with a cover letter; or (3) author and editor confer over the telephone or in person about possible story ideas; or (4) an editor phones a writer to propose a specific article topic.

Of my own nonfiction pieces published between 1981 and 1986, 60 percent fell into the first category, 15 percent into the second and 25 percent into the third. Since unsolicited assignments by definition lie beyond the writer's control, I don't offer advice here about the fourth kind of author/editor contact. And because editors confer mainly with writers whose work they already know, I concentrate on the first two categories—query letters and direct submissions. For beginners, these are the ways to break in.

Most of the time you should approach a publication via a query letter. Why? This strikes many newcomers to freelance writing as peculiar. Wouldn't a completed article be a better demonstration of your abilities than a letter? That's not the way editors look at it. For one thing, query letters save an editor time. Because a good query letter distills the focus, slant and tone of a proposed article in one captivating page, an editor can tell from a quick read whether or not a particular proposal deserves further thought. A harried editor with a few moments to spare would more profitably sort a stack of letters than attack that pile of unsolicited manuscripts.

But more important, a query letter gives the editor a chance to help shape an idea to suit her publication. If you ask (more elegantly, of course), "Hey, how about a profile on Mary Smith-Smith, the founder of Bio Tech in Cambridge, with photographs?" the editor has the opportunity to reply, "Yes, and don't forget, we publish for twenty-five- to thirty-four-year-old women entrepreneurs, most of whom never finished college, and we need 1,500 words plus a 300-word sidebar on what biotechnology is by November 2 for our February issue; no photos." If instead you submitted a completed profile of Smith-Smith, the same editor *might* reply, "Very interesting, except it's way too long, doesn't mention her personal life and assumes too much scientific knowledge. Could you rewrite it?" But that's unlikely. By submitting the manuscript instead of a query you've marked yourself as a novice, and many novices bristle at criticism or don't know how to redraft or cut. The more inundated an editor is with high-quality queries, the more unlikely she is to try to get a publishable rewrite from an inexperienced author. Seasoned writers query, and you have a much better chance of joining their ranks if you do too.

Yet will editors really take a chance and invite an unknown writer to submit an article merely on the basis of a letter? The sheer number of queries many publications receive seems daunting. *Cosmopolitan,* for example, reportedly receives fifty queries or manuscripts each day, or about 12,500 per year. But the numbers, whatever they are, don't tell the whole story. Twice editors at magazines that received a healthy excess of queries told me privately that they can't find enough good, dependable writers who understand their magazines' needs. A good portion of the material they receive is vague, sloppy, ungrammatical or on topics clearly outside the scope of the magazine. When they do assign articles to skillful writers who seem to promise what they want, the resulting articles sometimes come in late or never, or are lifeless, unsubstantiated or differently focused than the query. Consequently they really do open their mail hoping to find a gem of an offer from someone who might eventually become a treasured regular contributor.

Although querying should become your general practice, some ideas call for an alternate strategy. For any article whose effect depends on humor, submit the whole manuscript. This is because it's difficult to tell from a summary or even a sample of a humorous article whether the whole thing will be funny. For short (less than 1,200 words) opinion or personal-experience pieces, you may also submit the completed piece instead of querying. And for multiple submissions—for example, of short travel articles—to newspapers in non-overlapping circulation areas, you can usually submit the complete manuscript. I cover these and a few other exceptional cases in Chapter 4.

As important as it is to have a good idea and to present it well, it's just as important to find a publication that can use the article you're dreaming up. Sometimes, of course, the consummate outlet dawns on you along with the idea, but it's vital to make sure your hunch is sound. I've found that nonwriters' notions of appropriate markets sometimes reveal complete naiveté or wild misconceptions about how magazines work.

After I returned from a year working in China, I spent another year culling promising article ideas from my experiences and pitching them to various magazines and newspapers. When I talked with acquaintances in and around where I was living—Haydenville, Massachusetts—about what I was doing, I often got this response: "Try *New England Monthly!*" In reply I could only blink and change the subject. A slick regional magazine, *New England Monthly* not only restricts its coverage to events and situations in Connecticut, Rhode Island, Massachusetts, Vermont, New Hampshire and Maine, it even charges people who live outside those six states more to subscribe. *New*

England Monthly would be no more likely to run an article about China than the *New England Journal of Medicine* would be to accept a piece on how to start a dry cleaning business. My advisers, with all their good intentions, apparently assumed that *New England Monthly* was a good bet for my articles on China because I lived in New England—in fact, the magazine's offices were right around the corner from me; or that if an article were only well written enough, any magazine would snap it up.

Unfortunately, neighborliness and good writing in and of themselves move few, if any, magazine editors to buy and run material. Every magazine—even the most general—has a particular readership, "flavor" and scope. Recognizing this, many authors advise would-be freelancers to begin by "studying the markets" to figure out what editors are buying and then concoct ideas along exactly the same lines. That's not my approach. Between writing in willful ignorance of the marketplace (which rarely works), and crafting clones of what has already been published, lies a middle ground.

FINDING THE RIGHT ANGLE

Throughout this book I assume that you have a subject already in mind. The next step is to match your original idea with a particular publication (or two or three) by pondering the question "Who might want to read about this subject now—and why?" In the lingo, you thereby come up with an "angle" (or "slant") for your story. The idea is not to distort your material, but to focus it.

Here's an actual example. In late 1981, in an "eco-feminist" newsletter, I came across an isolated reference to "Ellen Richards, who founded the science of ecology." If that was true, I wondered, why hadn't I ever heard of this woman? At the library, I turned up a lot of interesting information about Richards, including the fact that she had graduated from and taught at Vassar. Because my sister had gone to Vassar, I knew the college had a well-produced alumnae magazine. But *Writer's*

Market, the standard guide to magazine markets (see Chapter 17 for details), didn't list it, and I couldn't quickly get a copy from my sister. At the least, I needed the magazine's actual title and the name of its editor. So I called up Vassar and asked for the alumnae magazine. "Hello, can you tell me the name of the present editor of the magazine?" I said to the woman who answered the phone. "I'm the editor. Mindy Aloff," she replied. "Can I help you with something?"

Since I had the editor on the line I plunged ahead. "Well, I was going to write you a query about an article about Ellen Swallow Richards . . ." "Yes, class of 1870, she started the home economics movement," Aloff interrupted in a tone of voice that implied, "How boring." "Yes, that's one thing she's known for, but she was trained as a chemist," I shot back. "She made some important discoveries about water quality and air quality, and she crusaded against indoor and outdoor pollution." I reeled off a few of her other achievements. "I'm interested in portraying her in the light of today's environmental feminism." "Hmm," said Aloff. There was a brief silence. "Hmm. Could you send me a query letter based on what you just said and some samples of your writing? It sounds interesting." I followed up and got the assignment. "Earth, Air, Water, Hearth: The Woman Who Founded Ecology" appeared in the Spring 1982 *Vassar Quarterly.*

As with that article, adroit angling often makes the difference between getting a "yes, please" or a yawn from an editor. When I teach freelance writing, I spend at least an hour on the following exercise. Class members suggest topics they're interested in. I choose one and together we do a little brainstorming, systematically going through the major headings in *Writer's Market* and discussing how to angle that topic for publications in each category. By the time we reach the trade magazines, everyone has had a dramatic demonstration of the great range of opportunities presented by appropriate angling.

One of my students, for an example, wanted to write about "maple die-off," a plague threatening New England's sugar maples. Under the heading "Association, Club and Fraternal" we would find magazines like *Kiwanis* and *The Rotarian*, with which he could take an approach that showed how citizens' groups were helping scientists and local governments solve the problem. For regional magazines under "Business and Finance," like *Boston Business Journal* or *The Business Times, for Connecticut Executives*, he could explain how "maple die-off" presented a long-term threat to fall foliage tourism—an angle also worth trying for travel trade magazines. The category "Career, College and Alumni" suggests the innumerable alumni magazines of New England colleges and two possible tacks: the involvement of that school's researchers in battling the plague, or how it was affecting trees on campus. A focus on the disease's threat to the world maple syrup supply might appeal to *Vegetarian Times* or *Whole Life*, listed under "Health and Fitness."

That's only the beginning. Other feasible headings include "Home and Garden" (alerting homeowners to symptoms of the disease), "In-flight" (airlines that serve New England), "Nature, Conservation and Ecology" (on whether the blight is caused by acid rain or road salt), "Regional," "Retirement," "Rural," "Science," "Travel" and some of the trade magazines under "Farm." Although these magazines would require different sorts of information to fill out an appropriate article, none would force the author to adopt a different attitude toward the problem than he would otherwise want to take.

This class exercise usually demonstrates another lesson as well: the importance of narrowing a topic to a manageable size. When you see the number of directions you can take with a seemingly narrow idea, it's much easier to comprehend that a topic alone doesn't constitute a focus for a piece. As I explain further in Chapter 7, you can't write a coherent article about "maple die-off" *per se;* you need an organizing principle that will tie together selected information about the subject. Practice in angling will help you convince an editor that you can produce a well-focused article.

For the Ellen Richards article, I knew that a Vassar publication would probably want a piece about a famous alumna if I could answer the question "Why run an article about her now?" The "why *now?*" criterion turns out to be even more crucial for newspapers. What makes the story newsworthy? Journalists call searching for a timely angle on a subject looking for a "news peg." Finding a news peg can be as simple as noting a first or hundredth anniversary or as complex and brainwracking as watching the news for trends or incidents you can somehow relate to your topic. During the year I spent writing articles about my experiences in China, a news peg, or lack of one, several times marked the difference between unsalable material and a story newspapers were eager to run.

I had masses of notes on daily life in China, on the government bureau where I worked and on topics like economic reform, religion and education in China. But I had only a little success interesting editors in "Typical Day in China" features. At first my efforts to publish something on a more focused topic—the nearly nonexistent Chinese legal system—flopped too. The editor of *Student Lawyer* liked my query letter on the subject but rejected the article. I guessed that the focus was off and rewrote it. She rejected it again. Fortunately my Chinese colleagues had given me a subscription to *Beijing Review* as a farewell present. One week it ran an article announcing a five-year campaign to publicize the function of the law; after working in that new information, I sold my piece on China's legal chaos to the *Christian Science Monitor*. Around the same time I read that the Chinese government had halved the Chinese workers' official two-hour lunch break. Suddenly I had a timely angle for a piece on siesta habits and entrenched traditions at my office. The *Boston Globe* op-ed editor accepted my 700-word article titled "China's Nap Reform."

ANALYZING YOUR INTENDED MARKET

In some other cases, finding a home for an idea may depend on coming up with an answer to "Why would *these* readers want to read about this subject?" This test may require careful investigation. One of my students wanted to write an article on how to travel through Europe with a young child, based on her experiences. She selected *Redbook* as her target magazine. According to the listing in *Writer's Market,* the "young child" part of her idea was apropos: "*Redbook* addresses young mothers between the ages of 25 and 44. More than half of *Redbook*'s readers work outside the home and have children under 18." But were *Redbook* readers of the class and income to consider taking a child to Europe? *Writer's Market* said nothing on this point. So how to determine whether or not her idea fell within the magazine's scope? She could have written and sent her query without knowing. She could have requested *Redbook*'s writer's guidelines, waiting for their return in her self-addressed stamped envelope. I suggested that if she spent an hour or two at the library analyzing the magazine, she would come up with as reliable an answer as she might ever get.

Analyzing a magazine's three or four most recent issues is the surest way to divine its peculiarities of scope, style and approach and to rule it out or in for a certain idea or angle. In the *Redbook* case, my student first had to scrutinize the articles about leisure activities and travel. Did the magazine stress day jaunts in the family car or airplane trips to distant destinations? Did service pieces explain how to buy and install a Jacuzzi or how to accumulate coupons to save pennies at the supermarket? Advertisements—products, slogans and settings—can often reveal even more than editorial content. The following section goes into great detail with another example.

If the analysis yields a negative conclusion, you'll have to begin hunting for a more suitable outlet. For the article on traveling in Europe with a toddler, city women's publications (like *New York Woman* and *Boston Woman*), parents' magazines, airlines' in-flight magazines and the travel sections of large metropolitan newspapers bear investigating. It doesn't make sense to restrict your search to publications you're familiar with; browse through the categories and listings in *Writer's Market,* haunt library periodical rooms and newsstands and rummage through magazine racks in waiting rooms and friends' houses to broaden your awareness of magazines beyond those you normally read or see.

Once you do find a plausible angle and a target publication for your idea, two more considerations demand your attention before you draft a query letter or prepare the article for submission. First, has your target publication run anything similar to your topic recently? Checking *Reader's Guide,* the microfilmed *Magazine Index* or the index (if one exists) to a newspaper can save you time, frustration and postage. Keep in mind that what a magazine considers "recent" will vary. An airline's magazine may run features on its hub city's best restaurants or museums once a year or even once an issue. At magazines like *Bride's* or *Baby Talk,* which can count on rapid turnover of readership, it might be safe to propose another article on double weddings or bonding with an adopted infant two years after an article on that topic. But at magazines like *Yankee,* with exceptionally loyal readers, editors may prefer to wait more than ten years before going back to a subject they've covered.

Second, is your article seasonal or tied to a particular future event? If so, then your timing matters. *Writer's Market* usually indicates how many months before the optimal publication date you should submit a time-bound article. Monthly magazines usually need at least three or four months "lead time"; some require twice as long. Newspaper feature sections require one to three months. If you are querying, figure in enough time for the magazine to reply and for you to research and write the article. Suppose, for example, January marks the fifth anniversary of Mary Smith-Smith's business; draft your query to a monthly magazine no later than July. Or, if you want to try fall foliage pieces for newspapers, plan your strategy by May or June.

SAMPLE MAGAZINE ANALYSIS

In the fall of 1987, I embarked on a program to improve my eyesight. With the guidance of an experienced "vision therapist," I halved my glasses prescription in only five weeks and continued to improve. I had been inspired by some midlife adventure articles in *Esquire:* William Broyles, a forty-year-old former editor of *Newsweek* and no skilled mountaineer, flew to Peru to climb the highest peak in the Western Hemisphere and confronted death; Edward McCabe, president of an advertising agency, retired at age forty-eight to enter the Paris–Dakar road rally, which with its grueling terrain and a gang of murderous bandits in the Sahara tested his stamina, wits and nerve. Might there be a man-against-nature challenge equally demanding but less macho, and cheaper? I chose an inner goal with an outward criterion of success: learning to see clearly.

From the outset I envisioned the article I wanted to write about my project: a first-person mind vs. matter story, a quest encompassing suspense, personal revelation, responsible medical information and mind-body insights. For such an article what would be a likely home?

Naturally I thought about health magazines and turned to the *Writer's Market* listing for *American Health,* a magazine I'd seen on newsstands and elsewhere but had never read or examined thoroughly. *Writer's Market* revealed several interesting things: 70 percent (quite enough) of the content came from freelancers; it preferred to work with "published/established writers" (fine—I'd even done pieces on acupuncture, chiropractors and private doctors in China); its scope included "holistic healing" (certainly my vision project fell under that); with circulation of one million, it paid $600 to $2,000 on acceptance for articles of 1,000 to 3,000 words (wonderful, wonderful). Somehow I missed this explicit phrase (my eyes weren't perfect yet!): "no first-person articles."

So off I trooped to the library to perform a detailed magazine analysis, both for my own practical need and as an exercise for this book. Here, interlaced with commentary, are the results.

American Health Magazine: Fitness of Body and Mind
Published ten times a year in New York City
Issues examined: July/August, September, October
and November 1987 (four issues)

1. *Overall visual impression.* First I scanned the issues to see what the covers, illustrations and ads might be able to tell me. Three out of four covers showed a woman and a man interacting and the fourth displayed Jane Fonda—plainly this was no dull medical journal. Both ads and editorial pages included imaginative layouts, with large, eye-catching artwork and photos. Several ads for specialized products—walking shoes, plaque removal machines, a shampoo specifically formulated to remove chlorine—indicated readers with robust disposable incomes. But as one would expect in a health magazine, food ads, particularly for low-calorie, low-salt, low-caffeine products, predominated, joined by ads for exercise machines and personal items like sanitary napkins, condoms, contraceptive sponges, pregnancy tests, antiperspirants, vitamins and painkillers. Among several multiracial baby-product ads, one stood out: for "Weeboks," high-fashion (and of course healthful) sneakers for toddlers. Another showed a man playing with a baby. I concluded that *American Health* readers were probably socially progressive men and women twenty-five to forty, in their peak childbearing and narcissistic years.

2. *Format.* Within the space of 120 to 160 pages, each issue contained six to eight feature articles, three or four of them on the issue's special theme, and countless short, snappy news items. An average of 2.5 sidebars accompanied each feature article.

3. *Length of feature articles (including sidebars).* This would have been easier to check had I brought along a ruler. Instead I used a library charge slip to measure roughly how many

"lengths" each feature article took up. I counted up several samples of text for the average number of words per "length" and finally multiplied to get very approximate word counts. I ran out of patience after two issues, but here are my figures: in one issue five articles ran about 3,000 to 3,400 words, one 1,100 and the last 1,800; in the other, two were about 3,300 to 3,600 words, one 2,300, one 1,400 and the last only around 600 words. I inferred that the magazine was more partial to long articles than its listing in *Writer's Market* indicated.

4. *Opportunity for freelancers.* I found the magazine's two-column masthead unusually heavy with names. Among nineteen "advisers" listed, eighteen had various advanced degrees after their names; there were also "contributing editors," "consulting editors" and "correspondents" in addition to staff writers and editors. Nevertheless, according to the bio notes, freelancers not listed on the masthead wrote 60 percent of those four issues' feature articles. The notes identified 70 percent of the feature-article authors as science, medical or sports writers or regular *American Health* contributors (only two were doctors). A nonspecialist in health, science or sports writing, then, had at least a theoretical chance at breaking into the magazine. In addition, only one article in four issues was excerpted from a book.

5. *Types of articles.* I had to invent some categories to generalize about the kinds of feature articles favored. Ten of the articles in the issues I studied were packed with recent research results; eight were more general journalistic pieces on health people, health places or health practices. Two reported the pros and cons of a current, unresolved debate. Six I classified as pure advice—though I should add that in almost every instance the other types included advice as well, even an article on the diet of our Paleolithic ancestors. Dishearteningly, only one personal experience piece appeared in the four issues, the winner of *American Health*'s annual "Body Story" contest. Indeed, only one sidebar (an anonymous account of arranging an AIDS test),

the one book excerpt (by a doctor) and the "Body Story" contest winner used the pronoun "I" at all! "You, you, you" instead dominated.

Here I had to give up on *American Health* as a possible outlet for the piece I had in mind, unless I submitted it to the contest (which would mean writing "on spec" and competing with hundreds of other people). But I pressed on to see if other aspects of the material indicated whether or not an impersonal, research-oriented piece on natural vision improvement might appeal to *American Health* editors.

6. *Tone of articles.* Despite the magazine's lively, anecdotal style, the articles I examined had a remarkably consistent objective and careful tone. Authors always attributed controversial positions or recommendations to named researchers or experts. In these issues spirituality seemed as taboo as political activism. I couldn't turn up any substantive editorials or editorializing—not even in an article on AIDS testing or in the editor's column, and only subtly at the end of an article on protecting yourself against secondhand cigarette smoke. Plainly the magazine tried to ground everything it published in recent research. Even more clearly, to interest the editors in any article on vision improvement I would have to come up with a slew of studies, experts or experiments testifying to a clear scientific basis for my improved eyesight.

7. *Content.* My final question: was nonsurgical, nontechnological vision improvement too "far out" a topic for the magazine in any case? Here I couldn't help relying on subjective impressions and beliefs. I consider myself relatively well informed about holistic healing and alternatives to traditional Western medicine and found the coverage of holistic/alternative healing in those four issues extremely tame. Although a few articles discussed visualization, they described techniques that had already moved into the American mainstream. An article on acupuncture contrasted Western (actually, American) research and Chinese ideas on acupuncture, implying that no

Chinese research on acupuncture came up to Western standards—highly parochial, from my point of view. My guess, finally, was that natural vision improvement, along with practices like home birth, homeopathy, and crystal healing, would be beyond the pale for *American Health.*

The above analysis, rigorous and systematic for the sake of this book, took me about four hours in the library. Normally a half-hour to an hour should be enough to rule a certain magazine in or out for a particular article idea. Here are a few other questions worth considering when you try this with topics of a different sort.

8. *Geographical area covered. American Health* stayed pretty true to the first word of the magazine's title. For a regional magazine, it may be crucial to learn the boundaries of its geographical coverage. In-flight magazines invariably print material only on cities and areas to which that particular airline flies.

9. *Political slant.* Submitting a pro-Sandinista editorial to the *National Review* or an anti-Israel article to *Commentary* would be a waste of paper, energy and postage. If you're not familiar with a magazine's political slant, check several issues; some publications print a range of viewpoints while others have a "party line." For controversial subjects, some magazines prefer the writer to take a position, while others prefer a balanced presentation of pros and cons.

10. *Peculiarities of style.* One trademark of *Cosmopolitan,* for example, is a breathy, confessional style heavy on italics. Another magazine may favor puns, particularly in article titles; articles in another may tend toward short paragraphs of one, two or three sentences.

11. *Readers' educational level.* Sometimes this will show up in a magazine's choice of topics as well as its style. When I tried to interest *New Woman* in an article on older women returning to college, an editorial assistant told me editors had decided the subject wasn't within the magazine's scope at that time.

12. *Photo credits.* If you're wondering whether or not you should offer in your query letter to take or arrange photos, you can sometimes tell by examining the photo credits. Do the photo credits list the names of writers, photo services or people on the magazine's masthead?

3 / The Query Letter

I once read, in the "Announcements" column of the local clas-
sifieds, a notice recruiting students for the New England School
for Nannies. "Hmm, I'm interested in finding out more about
that, and I'll bet other people would be too," I thought. So did
I sit right down, match up the idea with an appropriate magazine and fire off a query? No. How could I? I didn't know
anything about the school besides its name and location.

When you want to propose an article based on your own
experiences, querying usually involves simply choosing a market, angling the story appropriately and writing a tight, compelling letter. But as the *Vassar Quarterly* assignment showed, with
most other kinds of subjects there is one more preliminary step:
gathering some pertinent, persuasive facts.

Instead of going to the library, in the New England School
for Nannies case I called the number in the ad. In a ten-minute
conversation with the director, I found out why she had started
the school, the courses in the ten-week program, how much
graduates earned and who employed them. I also learned that
there were other new nanny schools in the United States, but
hers was the only licensed one in Massachusetts. Most important, I verified that the "nanny" title was not a gimmick and that
this local school represented a nationwide trend. I could now
make my query letter pointed and specific.

Another time, for a possible *Psychology Today* piece on
children's nuclear fears, I had to find out whether or not scientists had completed enough formal studies to support a re-

search-results article. Not only did I go to the library to look up the last several years of *Psychological Abstracts,* I also called the public information departments of the American Psychological Association and the American Psychiatric Association for names of their members presently researching that area. After several hours of work, I knew that at least half a dozen psychologists and psychiatrists were investigating children's reactions to the nuclear threat. You can bolster almost any query by including names of particular authorities you plan to interview for your article.

If your query would be strengthened by a few up-to-date statistics or facts, you can save time and frustration by calling or writing organizations with experts on staff or the latest figures readily at hand. When you inquire, identify yourself as a freelance writer and explain the focus and scope of your proposed article. Often as a way to get their point of view across to the public, the staff of professional and special interest groups will do half your research for you. For instance, for an article on older women students I did for *Ms.,* I wrote to several educational and women's organizations with a one-page list of questions. Both the American Association of University Women and the Council on Adult and Experiential Learning sent back pertinent books, pamphlets and photocopies of articles in obscure journals in addition to answers to my questions and a list of experts to contact. Check the *Encyclopedia of Associations,* which most libraries have, if you're not sure what organizations might have the information you need.

If your article will require the views and experiences of one certain person, as for a profile, you will want to put out feelers beforehand to make sure that person will cooperate. One freelancer I know secured a potentially profitable assignment to profile an inventor and then couldn't get the man to talk to her. Although it's possible to contrive a profile without an interview with the main character, usually this predicament means no article and an embarrassed, empty-handed writer.

The letter itself should be typed on a letterhead or plain

paper with your address and telephone number and the date at the top. Always address it to a specific person at the publication you have selected, not to "The Editor." Consult the current *Writer's Market* for the appropriate name, or, even better, check the magazine's current masthead—the list of staff and affiliated contributors usually placed within a page or two of the table of contents. Be aware that the person listed as "publisher" rarely deals directly with writers and that "contributing editors" are just regular contributors, not staff. People named as "editor," "associate editor," "assistant editor" or "managing editor" would be the appropriate recipients. As with a resume, the optimal length of a query letter is one page, single-spaced. And as with a resume, neatness counts—a lot. After all, in a sense you are applying for a job. Keep that in mind if you're inclined to find the following list of "do's" and "don't's" picky.

1. Never use onionskin or erasable paper (the former tears and the latter smudges too easily); 20-pound bond in white or cream is best. If you must use computer paper, make sure you remove the perforated edges carefully.

2. If your medium is a typewriter, the ribbon should be black and fresh enough to make crisp, dark text. If any letters come out splotchy or filled in, clean the keys.

3. Don't do query letters on a computer printer unless it is letter-quality or very nearly so, with clear, dark impressions and distinct, standard-sized *p*'s, *q*'s and *g*'s. Don't justify the right-hand margins. Elite and pica type (12-pitch or 10-pitch) both are fine.

4. Overall the letter should look attractive and inviting, with generous margins and without any prominent crossouts or messy corrections.

5. Always send a personalized, original letter—never a photocopy.

6. Enclose a business-size self-addressed stamped envelope ("SASE") for the editor's reply.

But what about the content? Obviously, content matters too. In only one page, or two at the most, you must:

- explain why your idea is appropriate for that publication now

- explain why you are the person to write the article

- impart the flavor and approach of the proposed piece

- mention the most relevant business details, such as when you can complete the article, its length, whether or not you can supply photos, and so on

Experienced freelancers have found different formats that work. Often I begin with a "teaser" paragraph, an anecdote or a colorful introduction that might serve as the opening of the article I am proposing. My next paragraph provides background and additional clues on how I will handle the topic. In the third paragraph I put forward my qualifications, including a selection of my publication credits. I end with a brief "hope to hear from you soon" paragraph. Other writers prefer to begin more directly, with "I'd like to propose a piece on ————." Then come two or three sentences of background on the topic, and "Here's how I'd handle it," which introduces the leading paragraph or two of the article, indented. They go on to present their qualifications and end with a "how about it?" paragraph. Either way, you also have the option of pulling out the major points you propose to make in a crisp, "bulleted" (marked and indented) list, as above. Somewhere in your letter include a handy one-sentence summary of your idea or a tentative and evocative title.

Your tone should be natural, not stiff or overly formal. Avoid begging ("Please give me this chance"), threatening ("If you don't jump at my proposal, then you don't know how to run a magazine") or apologizing ("I've never had anything published yet") in your letter. If you can't cite publication credits, then think of other kinds of credentials to present. Editors respect the authority of experience, so if you want to write an article about home wine-making and you have experimented with different methods and bottled and enjoyed the results for ten years, mention that.

Try to anticipate and head off any doubts or questions the editor might have about your proposal. If your subject is controversial, say whether you plan to take a position or not. If you're offering a new perspective on a well-covered subject, explain how your approach is fresh. If your topic might lend itself to gushy sentimentality or melodrama, state your intention of avoiding those pitfalls. In a query on my natural vision improvement (after the analysis reprinted in Chapter 2), for instance, I included the following sentence to show my willingness to take a critical attitude toward the techniques that had helped me: "I envision a lively, responsible article with information from vision experts interspersed with my own story."

Some editors like to see clips along with a query. Others, knowing that any one clip might have been heavily edited, put more stress on the query letter itself. If you want to send clips, choose one or two (no more than three, I think) most similar in subject area, tone and length to the article your query letter is proposing. A nicely written travel article won't prove your ability to handle a celebrity interview. A dry, technical article in an academic or professional journal will actually work against you when you're trying for a general-audience assignment. Instead of sending academic or professional clips, mention your credits only and polish the letter itself in a lively, concrete style. Never, of course, send your original clips unless you have many extras; some editors routinely send them back but others file them, circulate them in the office or toss them out. To save postage, I often simply cite my publication credits and add, "I would be glad to send on clips if you would like"; several editors have responded with postcards and calls asking for them.

Query letters, like flap copy or personal ads, are a genre in themselves. Don't expect to produce a masterpiece on the first draft. Write, then put your first attempt aside; later, slash, tighten and refine it. (See Chapter 7 for suggestions on rewriting.) The letter must demonstrate skill, sparkle and a professional attitude toward writing. I cannot overstress the importance of proofreading your query letter and redoing it if necessary to make it neat, clear and error-free. You need to impress on the editor your ability to deliver a professional product. If your letter shows a disregard for accuracy or detail, why should the editor suppose your article will be different? Probably the most fatal mistake is misspelling the editor's name. Don't sabotage yourself. See Chapter 8 for more on maintaining credibility.

After you finally mail the letter, don't haunt the mailbox waiting for a reply and don't fret that your query has fallen into a black hole. Each editorial office has an established procedure for dealing with queries. At smaller publications, the editor may set queries aside until after the hectic scrambling to meet the next issue's deadline. At some medium-sized publications, editors circulate the promising proposals and meet weekly or bi-weekly to discuss them. At the largest magazines, assistants sift editors' mail and write rejection letters for all but a tiny minority of submissions, which then sit and wait for a busy editor's attention. *Writer's Market* listings provide magazines' generally optimistic estimates of their response time. The places I query get back to me in, on average, five weeks.

When you finally receive the response, it will take one of the following four forms:

1. An impersonal rejection letter. This may mean that an editorial assistant summarily screened your query out. Or your query may have made it to a senior editor, who was too busy to personalize the rejection. Try not to draw conclusions about your ability and self-worth from this kind of reply; just try again elsewhere.

2. A personalized rejection letter. Experienced writers knock their heads at the story about the novice who gave up writing after receiving a printed rejection letter from *The New Yorker* with a scribbled "Sorry" at the bottom. She concluded she was no good, when in fact any kind of handwritten note or personal letter constitutes intentional encouragement. Any time you receive a personal response from a named editor, you should follow up with another query or submission that includes something like: "Thank you for your kind response to my previous query. Here's another . . ." If you're lucky enough to receive an explanation of why the editor rejected your idea, resist the urge to shoot back a cantankerous rejoinder. You won't change his mind, only make him roll his eyes and remember to put a form rejection in your SASE automatically next time.

3. An offer to look at your article on speculation. Until you can present evidence that you have actually produced professionally competent and appropriate articles, an editor interested in your query might ask you to write your piece "on speculation" ("on spec") instead of "on assignment." "On spec" means that you bear all the risk and costs of preparing the article; the publication promises only to consider it seriously. Few publications extend such invitations casually. If you are a beginner, this is a chance to prove yourself. Take the challenge seriously and you might soon be in a position to receive assignments. I deal with possible terms of assignments in Chapter 9, where I also discuss what to do if you've already been published and you're asked to write "on spec."

4. An assignment, written or phoned, with or without a formal contract. This is the best possible response, especially if the terms of the assignment please you. If not, negotiate. (More on this in Chapter 9.)

Actually, there is a fifth response: silence. What do you do if you've heard nothing, say, six weeks after you mailed your query letter? The safest tactic is to send a follow-up letter asking whether or not your query was received and enclosing another self-addressed stamped envelope. If you follow up with a phone call, you run the risk of antagonizing a slow, methodical editor. On the other hand, you may find yourself talking to a fast, methodical editor who never saw your query. In that case, be prepared to reel off your idea as persuasively as you wrote it. In fact, some freelancer friends of mine who often submit to newspapers regularly follow up by phone as soon as a week after submitting a query or article. They claim newspapers lose or misplace correspondence from freelancers inordinately often.

To head off the long, frustrating wait for a response, query by query, some prepare multiple queries, sending three or four customized letters at one time. Orthodox opinion on this is that it's ethical only if you say in your letter that yours is a simultaneous query. Maverick freelancers disagree, arguing that the risk of having all three or four editors reply with assignments is low enough to make multiple queries worthwhile. Besides, they say, if an editor calls you to make an assignment only to find a competitor has beaten her out, she might be angry for a moment but will get back to you all the more quickly the next time. Perhaps. The only advice I have on this dilemma is that if you do send out multiple queries, decide in advance what you'll do if the good luck/bad luck of multiple "yesses" strikes.

SAMPLE QUERY 1

I chose *In These Times,* a leftist biweekly, for this proposed article on women in China because its readers would probably share my initial assumption that China had already liberated women. For added impact, I wrote the query on Foreign Languages Press stationery and mailed it from China shortly before I came home. Notice that I include my teaching experience here and not in the second sample letter, where it's not relevant.

The article appeared as "China's Women Are Hobbled by Feudal Ideas, New Priorities" in the February 6–12, 1985, issue of *In These Times*.

SAMPLE QUERY 2

This was a "cold" query letter, to an editor who didn't know me or my work. Notice how detailed I made paragraphs two and three and again how I presented only the qualifications that would buttress my credibility for this article. I sent it (and letter 3) on my letterhead, which included my address and phone number.

Roth called me three months later to make the assignment, changing the angle somewhat (see the sample assignment confirmation in Chapter 9). The article appeared as "Editorial Style" in the April 1987 issue of *Personal Publishing*.

SAMPLE QUERY 3

Whereas with sample queries 1 and 2 I was fairly clear and detailed about the content of my proposed article and my attitude toward the subject, here I concentrated on establishing that a problem existed. I didn't know what results research would turn up, so in paragraph three I presented a long list of the sources I would consult.

Since the editor I had previously dealt with at *Ms.* had left the magazine, I called its editorial department, where Karen Fitzgerald took the call, to ask which editor I should send the query to. Although I don't mention it in the letter, I knew that *Ms.* had had a "special college issue" in October of previous years. I did make it just in time for the October 1987 *Ms.*, where the piece was titled "I Thought I Was a Terrific Teacher Until One Day . . . My Older Students Taught *Me* a Lesson."

SAMPLE QUERY 1

August 11, 1984

Jay Walljasper, Editor
In These Times
1300 W. Belmont Ave.
Chicago, IL 60657

Dear Mr. Walljasper:

Remember the heartwarming slogans from Chairman Mao's China like "Women hold up half the sky"? Well, here comes the bad news: in Deng Xiaoping's China, female infanticide is on the rise, women in high places are suggesting that women become full-time mothers, and quotas ensure that women remain a minority in foreign language institutes. In the year that I have been living and working in Beijing, what I have learned about women's place in Chinese society has disturbed me greatly and destroyed any illusions I might have had that socialism in China has liberated women.

I would like to write an article for you of a length of your choosing reporting some of the most striking things I have learned about the place of women in today's China and attempting a brief analysis.

My credentials: I used to be a professor at Smith College, teaching philosophy and women's studies. After that I became a freelance writer, publishing in such places as *Yankee, Ms., Psychology Today* and *In These Times* (an article on war tax resistors in, I believe, April 1982). Then came my year in China as a writer/editor for China's foreign language publishing house. Starting in mid-September I will be freelancing again.

Please use the enclosed self-addressed stamped envelope to let me know if you are interested in this article and if so on what terms. I look forward to hearing from you.

Yours,

Marcia Yudkin

SAMPLE QUERY 2

September 9, 1986

Stephen F. Roth, Managing Editor
Personal Publishing
54 Ludlow St.
New York, NY 10002

Dear Mr. Roth:

With desktop publishing, you can dispense with typesetters. But you will still need an editor. Why? The two key reasons are credibility and readability.

Many people think an editor's only functions are to check grammar and spelling and smooth out awkward prose. An editor can indeed correct errors that a spell-check program would miss, such as singular nouns with plural verbs or "it's" instead of "its." But editors are also experienced in catching the mistakes that destroy credibility, such as "Columbia" for "Colombia" or numbers that don't add up. More importantly, an editor will make consistent a myriad of small details. Most people have no idea that within each publication copy editors standardize when numerals are used and when numbers spelled out, whether or not a comma will follow the next-to-last item in a series, when italics or small capitals are used, and so on. But if a publication contains no such standardization, readers will feel uncomfortable without knowing why. Finally, it's very difficult to proofread material that one has written or typed and formatted oneself; an editor's experience and fresh eyes will prevent embarrassing slips in one's final product.

I'd like to write an article of 1,500 to 2,000 words urging desktop publishers to have an editor go over the product before the final printout. I can include two sidebars, one on how to find a qualified editor and the other a resource list for people who are determined to add editing to their list of self-publishing skills.

As a freelance writer, I have sold articles to *Yankee,* the *Boston Globe, Ms., Psychology Today* and many other national and regional publications. I also have extensive experience as a freelance editor. Recently I wrote and prepared a camera-ready copy of the *Guidebook for Publishing Philosophy* on computer for the American Philosophical Association.

May I write this article for you? If you would like to see clips I would be happy to send some along. I enclose a self-addressed stamped envelope for your response.

Yours,

Marcia Yudkin

SAMPLE QUERY 3

March 30, 1987
Ellen Sweet, Editor
Ms.
119 West 40th St.
New York, NY 10018

Dear Ellen Sweet:

With a declining pool of American 18-year-olds, an increasing number of American colleges and universities are welcoming or even recruiting older women students. But are these schools adapting their policies and practices to provide for the special needs of adult women students?

This question came to mind last fall, when I taught a feminism course at Smith College that consisted of one-third older women ("Ada Comstock Scholars" or "Adas") and two-thirds traditional-age students. Despite the Ada program's notable flexibility and financial aid, several Adas complained that the school's efforts to include them did not go far enough. Specifically, the Ada Center did not allow children, women with professional skills were offered on-campus minimum-wage employment as part of their financial aid, and the campus culture forbade children's presence in classrooms, although this was customary during vacations at a local community college. Even more dramatically, at the end of my course, most of the Adas and none of the traditional-age students revolted against the non-hierarchical course structure I had set up, leading me to suspect that the educational needs and preferences of 25-to 50-year-old women may differ from those of 20-year-olds.

For an article on how well American colleges and universities are accommodating and nurturing their increasing numbers of older women students, I propose to interview older women students and support staff at women's colleges (where the former now constitute about one-fifth of the student population), community colleges that may specifically attract poorer and minority women, and large universities that have no special programs at all for older women. I would also speak with psychologists who have studied women's development and educational psychology. This article would probe a recognized trend more deeply than anything I have yet seen in print.

I'm writing to you at the suggestion of Karen Fitzgerald; previously I dealt with Ruth Sullivan for a book review in *Ms.* in 1982 and my "Falling in Love in China" last year. I've done many research-and-synthesis pieces for national magazines of the type I'm now proposing, most notably an April 1984 cover story on children's nuclear fears for *Psychology Today.*

I look forward to hearing from you.

Yours,

Marcia Yudkin

4 / Direct Submissions

I've stressed that in most cases you should query an editor rather than submit a completed manuscript. But there are five instances when direct submissions may be or are definitely appropriate. First, humor pieces, for reasons explained in Chapter 2. Since I don't write humor (at least not intentionally), I don't have anything further to say about this case beyond general encouragement. The ability to make people laugh, especially without disparaging other people, is a gift that editors cherish even more than the average person. If you have that flair, good luck.

Second, short travel articles or feature articles can be offered as completed pieces to newspapers with non-overlapping circulation areas. Essentially this is scattershot marketing. Instead of extending exclusive offers one by one and waiting until you can tailor the product to a definite customer, you create the product and fire it off in many different directions at once. Count on at least several shots of your fusillade missing. Some newspapers take few or no freelance articles and some that do may be overstocked. Other papers may have just covered your topic or consider it too exotic for their readers. If you've written a narrative travel article, papers that run only destination pieces will refuse it. If yours is a destination piece, those that prefer narratives will say no. Still, you hope that at least one or two out of ten grab your submission as exactly what they want. Some people succeed with this approach, just as some hunters bag prey by raking the forest with bullets. You may conclude that the percentage of shots that will inevitably miss their targets doesn't warrant the effort of writing the article, copying it and addressing and licking all the envelopes.

The third case represents your best opportunity to sell a completed article and one of the best ways for a beginner to break into print. Many magazines reserve special columns for personal-experience or opinion pieces, often paying well and providing authors with an extraordinary showcase. For years *Redbook* has solicited contributions for its "Young Mother's Story" series (and pays $750 at this writing), while the *New York Times Magazine* has "About Men" ($1,000), *Glamour* an opinion column called "Hers" or "His" ($1,000), *Newsweek* "My Turn" ($1,000) and so on. Many magazines, like *Writer's Digest*, *Smithsonian* and *Women's Sports and Fitness,* run the open column on their last page. Most newspapers have an "op-ed" page (*op*posite the *ed*itorial page), but there you'll want to check several issues to make sure all contributors aren't either regular columnists or employees of that newspaper.

Almost all of these columns have a very rigid word length. Most must fit on one page in the magazine's usual type size, leaving room for the headline, the author's bio note and sometimes an illustration. If *Writer's Market* doesn't list the word limit, count up the number of words in one sample column, round that off to the nearest hundred and trim your submission to that length, plus or minus fifty words. Most magazine columns run 900 to 1,200 words and newspaper columns 700 to 1,000 words, but don't take my estimate as your guide; check.

Not only must an open-column submission be the required length; it must be highly polished and tight. Strange as this may sound to novices, short articles frequently require more effort and skill than long ones. One botched description and a few weak transitions may spoil an entire short piece; a blurry focus kills it. Three sentences that don't belong may comprise 8 percent of the total content. Remember, competition is stiff. Feedback from alert friends and fellow writers may spell the difference between acceptance and rejection here. I usually agonize through three, four or even five drafts, sometimes over a period of months, before I feel confident that my short article says precisely what I want to say in an interesting, artful and persuasive way.

Before you put all that work into a contribution for a specific column, make certain that your chosen subject and slant will suit your target publication and that you are an eligible contributor. Generally this will involve knowing your target. It wouldn't work to submit an editorial condemning capitalism to most American business magazines or a defense of school-board censorship to "The Last Word" of *The Progressive*. A medical magazine may reserve its open column for doctors who want to sound off; the *New York Times Magazine* accepts "About Men" pieces only from men.

Fourth, when an article that you've written on spec or on assignment is rejected, you may want to send it right off, complete, to a competing publication. I say "may want to" because this isn't really what you *should* do. You *should* go back to the query stage, angle your subject for your next target and present the idea as if the article isn't written (rewriting it later if that seems necessary). Yet when a commissioned or requested article is rejected, I can rarely summon the energy to write another appealing query letter. Faced with a choice between letting a good article languish on my desk and sending the damned thing right out again, I've sometimes chosen the latter, and I've sold at least two articles doing so. A similar dilemma arises when you've written an article in a white heat of inspiration and believe it's good. You can send it out as is, send queries for it around, or as Dan Okrent, editor of *New England Monthly,* once suggested, "write the editor that you've written such and such an article and can you send it to him? If I say yes, that means I'm promising to take a very serious look at the article."

Finally, when you've retained resale rights (see Chapter 9), you should submit the article, either in your original manuscript form or in its published form, to other magazines that consider previously published submissions. *Reader's Digest* and the *Utne*

Reader buy reprint rights for mainstream or progressive articles, respectively; a good hunt through *Writer's Market* will turn up other markets, including syndicates, willing to take articles from other publications.

Along with any complete-manuscript submission, include a short (half-page or less) personalized cover letter presenting yourself and what you've enclosed. Mention your qualifications and experience, the subject of the article and why your article is topical now. If you have or can obtain photographs and illustrations to accompany the article, describe them, but you needn't send them at this point. If the article was previously published, say where and what rights the original outlet purchased. A cover letter should meet the same strictures of neatness and presentation (paper, type, margins, etc.) as a query letter.

Double-space the manuscript itself on ordinary white medium- or heavy-weight paper, with type on only one side of the page. Normally sending a clear photocopy is fine. On the first page, either in the upper right- or upper left-hand corner, supply the following information:

> Your name
>
> Your address
>
> Your phone number
>
> Approximate word count for the article
>
> Rights you are offering (see Chapter 9)
>
> Your social security number

Most paying publications will need your social security number because they must furnish the IRS with a list of contributors to whom they paid more than a certain amount of money per year. Putting the number right on the manuscript helps ensure that your payment will not be held up.

Below the corner heading, skip a few lines and center your title in all capitals. Skip a few more lines and start the article proper. Don't justify the right-hand margins or hyphenate if you're using a computer or electronic typewriter. If your article contains definite sections which will call for page breaks or white space, indicate them with several centered asterisks. My first published short story might have been more of a thrill for me had I done that. I merely left extra white space in my manuscript where I wanted page breaks in the story, but the layout person didn't notice or ignored them, destroying the coherence of what I had written. If your article ends at the bottom of a page, indicate the end with "-end-" or "-30-" or a few asterisks, so the editor and typesetter won't wonder whether they've lost the rest of the manuscript. Head each page following the first with your last name and the page number. Fasten the pages of the article together with a paper clip; don't use staples or add a cover as if it were a college term paper. Be sure to tear apart the accordioned pages that come out of your computer printer.

Enclose a self-addressed stamped envelope for the editor's reply. With multiple submissions or reprint offers you may omit the SASE, telling the editor to throw the article out if it's not acceptable, or enclose instead a stamped, self-addressed post-card with "No thanks" or "Yes, we'd like to buy it" responses the editor can check off. Never send irreplaceable photos to a newspaper unless they are specifically requested. Expect the reply time to a manuscript submission to be slightly to very much longer than for a query.

SAMPLE COVER LETTER

Here I broke the rule about never submitting to "The Editor." My submission did get to the right person, who called me to tell me he planned to run it. (In Chapter 12 I'll tell you what later happened to the article, titled "China's Nap Reform.")

In my cover letter (on my business stationery) I briefly explained the "news peg" for the article and my qualifications to comment on China.

SAMPLE COVER LETTER

December 21, 1984

Op-Ed Editor
The Boston Globe
135 Morrissey Blvd.
Boston, MA 02107

Dear Editor:

I was astounded when I read recently that Chinese office workers' nap times will be curtailed after the turn of the year. From September 1983 to September 1984 I worked as a writer/editor for one of the government offices that will be affected, the Foreign Languages Press in Beijing. Enclosed is my comment for your op-ed page.

Before I went to China, I was a freelance writer publishing in places like the *Village Voice, Ms.,* the *New York Times* and *Psychology Today.* While in China I wrote *Making Good: Private Business in Socialist China,* which will appear in 1985. I am now working on a book entitled *The Gates of Friendship,* about my experiences in China.

Because of the timely nature of this article, if I don't hear from you by Wednesday, January 2, I will offer it elsewhere. If you call me before then I will be happy to discuss any changes you might think necessary.

I look forward to your reply.

Yours sincerely,

Marcia Yudkin

5 / Informational Interviewing

I once read an entire book on interviewing and finally threw it aside as useless. Like many nonwriters, the author saw the two parties in each interview as hunter and prey, the best interviewers cornering and trapping their natural adversaries into exposing themselves. But I do that kind of interviewing very rarely, and unless you aim to be the next Bob Woodward or Barbara Walters, so will you. Keep in mind that whenever you ask anyone for information or an opinion, you are interviewing. Most articles require you to draw out of people what they know, think or feel. Yet even when they would like to cooperate, people often don't explain completely, vividly or specifically. As interviewer you must then coax from them the details that will make your article glow.

Imagine, for example, interviewing divorced middle-class women who had to apply for welfare after the ex-husbands stopped sending child support payments. *Compare the story you could construct after this interview:*

Q: How would you describe the experience of applying for welfare?

A: Humiliating. It was the most humiliating experience of my life.

Q: Would you have avoided going there if you could?

A: Of course.

—with what you could write after this:

Q: What was it like to apply for welfare?

A: Humiliating. It was the most humiliating experience of my life.

Q: What kinds of questions did they ask you?

A: Whose fault the divorce was, could I go back to my parents, did I have a live-in boyfriend.

Q: What was the case worker's attitude?

A: Bored. Accusing.

Q: Why was he—was it a "he"?

A: No, it was a twenty-one-year-old girl wearing a cashmere sweater and gold bracelets. I'm sure the little snit thought *she* would never end up abandoned and unemployed. I wanted to give her a little lecture about life.

Q: Why didn't you?

A: Because she had a little checklist of things to ask me, she kept looking at her watch, and she never once really looked me straight in the eye.

Q: What would you have said in your lecture?

And so on. The secret is to keep probing for details, color, examples, anecdotes. I've noticed that people tend to offer summaries and judgments when you ask them to reminisce or describe their experiences. Usually I have to keep asking things like, "For example—?" and "What do you mean?" to get them down to the specific basis for their generalizations and attitudes. People are often loath to exhume the details, the raw data, because this forces their memories uncomfortably close to the emotions they originally felt. With less personal material, officials may try to satisfy you with talk like "a few," "most," "previously," instead of exact dates, quantities and percentages that may take some time to look up. Analogously, some experts assume their general conclusions deserve more attention than do particular examples. Probe as if your article depends on your clarifying every vague remark—for it does.

Not only will the details help you breathe life and authenticity into your story, they also enable you to present your material in a way that allows readers to draw their own conclusions. The second interviewer, above, can *show* the reader what happened and let her decide whether or not welfare personnel and policies are avoidably intrusive; the first can only provide the abstract, almost question-begging label "humiliating." If you didn't follow up after the director of Belles Hills Social Services said, "A shocking number of middle-class abandoned housewives came through our office in 1987," you have only the director's opinion or reaction, not the facts. To gather material for a first-rate, persuasive article, then, you have to be willing to prod and annoy your sources a little.

That's not the same as confronting an adversary, however. More likely, you'll have to ask questions that sound naive or even dumb. If you don't understand the director's explanation of why those housewives couldn't walk out with food stamps so that they could feed their children, keep asking. Once in a great while you will have to challenge an interviewee. When I interviewed a Wellesley College dean for my *Ms.* article on older women students, I asked her whether or not older students learn differently from younger ones and hence require different educational approaches. With great enthusiasm, she explained why older women thrived at women's colleges. I stopped taking notes, scratched my head and suggested that she hadn't answered my question. "You know, it's an interesting question," she replied, and confessed that she wasn't certain of the answer. An hour later, she told me I was a good interviewer; clearly she hadn't felt I was her enemy. Sometimes, on the other hand, you'll do best to simply scratch the entire interview. In China I interviewed an old private barber who seemed to be hiding something in his background. The dates, occupations and reasons he gave for moving from job to job didn't add up and

sounded more suspicious the more I probed. To the befuddle-
ment of my escorts, I suddenly closed my notebook, thanked
the barber and went early to my next appointment.

You can often trace mistakes in articles based on interviews
to a reporter's failure to ask for clarifications. My friends who
have been profiled in local newspapers have told me about
mistakes that apparently stemmed from reporters' assumptions.
The owner/designer of a nursery and show garden found her
head gardener referred to as a "co-owner." Probably she had
used the word "partner" in talking about their creative collaboration on the garden, and the reporter assumed she meant
"business partner." A cartoonist found himself credited with a
master's degree from the local university instead of just a bach-
elor's. He had probably used the word "degree," and the reporter assumed that he meant "graduate degree." Don't take
anything for granted.

This is easier said than done, but practice helps. In fact,
interviewing demands almost as much adeptness and concentration as tightrope walking. While listening carefully, you must
also be assessing what you hear for vagueness or logical holes.
At the same time, you're half formulating your next question
and thinking of the overall purpose of the interview. If you're
a talkative sort, you have to restrain the urge to voice your own
opinion and experiences. Meanwhile you're usually taking
notes, and sometimes you're also trying to catch the speaker's
tone and body language and observe the surroundings. If this
sounds intimidating, I suggest you practice with the tightrope
only inches above the ground, by interviewing a friend or family
member about some event or process they know about and you
don't, writing it up and checking back with them to see how well
you've communicated what they know.

Preparation helps immensely too. I always draft a list
beforehand of questions or areas to ask about, although I may
not refer to the list until the interview is almost over. If I'm
unfamiliar with the subject I'm writing on, I'll do some reading
to help me formulate focused questions. Or I'll conduct a back-

ground interview, a long, exploratory conversation with someone who can orient me. Like the library research, this gives me clues to the important themes I should touch on when I really get going. For instance, the first thing I did after *Ms.* assigned me an article on older women students was to get together, woman to woman, with a thirty-five-year-old student I knew. During our more-than-hour-long talk, I took no notes except the name and number of someone she thought I should interview. Afterward I jotted down some of the motifs she dwelled on: grade anxiety, low self-esteem, the prickliness of the older women students from working-class backgrounds. Although I never quoted her in the article, her input was just as vital as my formal interviews, because she helped me figure out what to ask.

How you'll word your questions and structure the interview demands some thought ahead of time as well. I recommend beginning by restating the focus of your article, then asking for identifying details about the interviewee—full name, title, occupation, age, hometown, etc. Then go after specific facts and figures you may need. Later you pose more open-ended questions such as, for the women on welfare, "How would *you* change the welfare system if you were in charge?" This strategy helps put your source at ease and ensures that you get the hard facts before you fish around for insights, quotes and anecdotes. When you think you're done, ask, "Is there anything you feel is important that I've missed?" and "Is there anyone else you think I should talk to?" Don't rush to fill every moment of the interview with words; a stretch of silence can give your subject's thoughts a chance to jump around productively. Throughout, avoid two-part or three-part questions and those that can be answered simply "Yes" or "No"; the former confuse people and the latter often bring the flow of talk to a dead halt.

So far I've said nothing about the setting or mechanics of interviews. Must you always interview someone in person? For my *Psychology Today* article and several others, how people looked and acted while they talked was irrelevant, so I gathered all my information by phone. The most important rule in phone-interview etiquette, I think, is never call someone "cold" and try to carry on the interview then. Instead identify yourself, explain what your article is on and for whom and then say, "I'd like to ask you some questions about ———, and I don't think it'll take more than ———minutes. Can we set up a convenient time to talk?" When you let busy people know that you respect their crowded schedules, they do usually find ten or fifteen minutes somewhere in their week. And by specifying the topic in advance, you give them the chance to gather documentation or prepare some thoughts.

Consider also interviewing by mail when, on a low or nonexistent phone budget, you want your article to have a national scope. Arrange your in-depth interviewing close to home and mail letters containing no more than two or three evocative questions to other sources far away. Although you'll lack the give-and-take and follow-up you can have locally, you may very well elicit quotable anecdotes or opinions that you can integrate into your article to make it seem as if you flew around or at least called around the country to gather information. Enclose a self-addressed stamped envelope to increase your chances of a reply.

I've left the most vexing issue in interviewing almost till last: to tape-record or not to tape-record? Up to now, whether I've interviewed over the phone or in person, I have never used a tape recorder. Recently I've learned that both William Zinsser and Gay Talese, punctilious and sophisticated reporters, share my bias. My reasons are as follows. First, transcribing tapes takes an inordinate amount of time. Even a fast typist with a transcribing machine needs about two hours to transcribe a one-hour tape. Unless you plan to use a high percentage of the interviewee's exact words, that's two hours largely wasted. Secondly, you must always take notes anyway if you do tape-record—the machines can fail to work without your knowing. And finally, from years of being in school, I can take down the gist of what someone is saying accurately and quickly. According to journalism professor Shirley Biagi, the average person speaks 100 words a minute, but much is repetition, filler or information that would go into your article as background in *your* voice, not the subject's. That is, usually you're not going to write, " 'I was born in Atlanta,' said Edgar Johnston, 'in 1938,' " but something more like "Southern-born Johnston, now 50, . . ." Hence scrawling down "b. '38, Atla" is quite good enough.

Instead of a tape recorder, I use a clipboard with paper in it, and a pen. I summarize much of what I hear and put down exact words only from time to time, when the color or authenticity of what I'm hearing seems important. I add quotation marks in my notes so when I get home I'll know which are my words and which the interviewee's. Sometimes I do get jammed up when trying to get it all down at the same time that I'm trying to decide on the next question, but I've found: (1) People often spontaneously slow down, repeat themselves or just wait when they see me writing, writing, writing after they've stopped talking, and (2) If they don't, I can catch up by rewording and repeating a question I've already asked.

On the other hand, the time lag does sometimes create awkward moments during phone interviews, when the person I'm talking with can't *see* that I'm struggling madly to keep up. I've had to mutter inane things like, "Just a minute, I'm getting . . . this . . . down. . . ." Recently I've heard of a device called a "telephone recording control" that connects a tape recorder to a telephone, which would allow me to set up a tape recorder as a backup for those sticky times. As I understand it, so long as I explain to my interviewee that I'm doing this, it's legal. I think I will look for that device and try it out.

Also, I would turn to a tape recorder in a legally sensitive situation, if I was dealing with a very fast talker from whom I needed long quotes, or if I had to interview someone in a dark, moving car. Freelancers I know who do routinely use a tape recorder say that it enables them to look the other person in the eye during the interview and later helps them recreate important moments. They warn, however, that you should always set off with fresh batteries and use a machine with a battery indicator. Coming home from an exhilarating interview and finding the tape blank is every writer's nightmare. It does happen. You can help stave off disaster by taking notes even when the machine seems to be working fine.

Journalistic dogma, I know, is never to let an interviewee see your article before it is published. But if you've interviewed in a field in which you're not particularly knowledgeable, it's often in everyone's interest for you to call subjects back to read back their quotes and what you've written based on what they said. You may have substituted the wrong synonyms for technical terms the expert used, or the expert may catch a mistake or something misleading that she did actually say during the interview. As I said at the outset, I consider most interviewing a cooperative process; failing to weed out inaccuracies serves no one.

When I write up quotes for my article, I usually feel free to "cut and paste" together things said at separate times and to reword for grammatical smoothness. My goal is to make someone's point of view or information as clear as possible. Since my run-in with *Screw* (see Chapter 8), I've never had anyone complain about being misquoted.

6 / Constructing an Article

From a high school or college English teacher you may have learned to organize an essay by first announcing what you're going to say, then saying it, and finally repeating what you've just said. Forget that advice. If you've learned, formally or on the job, to write news stories, forget that too. News stories need to be written so that the end may be snipped off without losing anything vital. In contrast, the general structure for magazine articles and most newspaper features runs like this:

lead—background—development—close

Briefly, the lead grabs the reader's attention with a striking incident, fact or quote connected to the main subject of the article. The background paragraph or paragraphs put the lead into context with the essential facts the reader needs to appreciate the incident, fact or quote. The development develops the subject and the close winds up the article with a memorable anecdote, observation or quote.

In addition, the kind of article I'm discussing is not pure information or chronology; it has a *theme,* a main point that can be summed up in one sentence. Many magazines put the theme right in an article's title, subtitle or blurb. For example, here are some titles from the October 1986 *Ms.:* "Architecture on a Human Scale: Joan Goody's Designs Give a Small-Town Feel to Urban Space"; "A Better MBA: There's More to Business than Numbers-Crunching" and "A Mother Confronts Her

Daughter's Scoliosis." In the October 1986 *Atlantic* the blurb for the article "How Business Is Reshaping America" ran as follows: "Metropolitan areas are turning into clusters of inter-dependent 'urban villages'—mini-downtowns surrounded by low-density housing. The phenomenon has changed the way millions of Americans live and work."

Notice in the first case that the theme is not merely "Joan Goody's architecture" but a distinct point about it. In the last case the theme is much more specific than "The way urban Americans live and work is changing." As I hinted in Chapter 2, a mere topic doesn't provide sufficient focus for an article. In addition to the topic, you also need an angle on the topic, a particular attitude toward it. Composition teachers sometimes call the theme the "controlling idea" of an essay. I think of the theme as a spine for a creature you hope to create on the page. You needn't blatantly expose the spine, but unless you put one there and make sure that all the matter you add adheres to it, you'll have something both shapeless and inert, not an entity with a distinct, living identity.

Besides the theme, you'll also need the lead before you start writing. As most writing manuals explain, leads come in many varieties—anecdotal, provocative, atmospheric; a summary, a question, a quotation and so on. All represent viable article openings; my own favorite is the anecdotal lead. To draw readers in, I like to introduce a subject with a striking human incident or situation whose significance is not entirely clear. The small human drama tugs on them: what does it mean? They read on for background and development and by the end, if I've achieved my purpose, they've understood something about a subject they may not even have thought they'd be interested in.

Since the lead is crucial to the success of your article, don't worry if its selection causes you agony. Occasionally as early as the query stage I've come up with something that feels perfect. More often when I've finished gathering all my information I have to reread my notes several times, looking for compelling quotes, interesting angles, revealing incidents, startling images or observations. Then I'll put the material aside for a day or two to let ideas percolate up from my subconscious. It's hard for me to analyze this aspect of writing, but I think one consideration in my screening of possible leads is whether or not I can see a way to echo the beginning at the end. For many articles, an ideal beginning is one that I can circle back to with new insight. Also, I like to design pieces that will leave images, questions and contrasts in the reader's mind.

If, like me, you don't sit down to write your article until you've got the lead roughed out in your head, you're much less likely to suffer the infamous "terror of the blank page" (or, nowadays, "blank screen"). Once the lead is polished, the struggle becomes more manageable problem solving—how to keep the focus clear, how to slip fluidly from point A to point B. I write slowly and tinker as I go along. Since every article presents different technical challenges, and since I seem to figure out how to meet them in a nonverbal part of my brain, I don't have much general advice to offer about shaping the long middle of an article. I do recommend that you finish gathering material before you write. Reporters often draft an article with holes labeled "TK" (for statistics and names "to come"), but how can you know that when you call for the figures or specific cases, you won't learn something that throws off your basic argument? Fairly detailed notes will also help for articles based on your own experience rather than research. To generate those notes, try brainstorming, writing a letter to a friend or speaking into a tape recorder.

I don't always have an ending in mind when I start. And if anything, I'm more fussy about closings than about openings. An article's conclusion is one's chance to give the reader a final, memorable impression, whether that be a philosophical remark, a prediction or a push to action. Not only do I search for a suggestive closing quote, metaphor or fact, I labor to convey it in the proper tone and rhythm. To me, ending an article is very much like winding up a piece of music. Trailing into an off-key warble or some gawky notes won't do. Instead I want to cadence to a resolution, swoop into a graceful rising note or slow the pace to a low, definite accent.

Drawing up an outline of sorts before writing is usually a good idea. For longer articles, I may not use more than a checklist of points I want to work in, along with the lead. For shorter articles, I tend to be much more rigorous. For the *Ms.* back-page article included in the next chapter, I had to dramatize in only 900 words how my forbidden romance in China changed me. I figured that meant eight paragraphs of slightly more than 100 words each. With one for the lead, one for background and one for the close, that left only five paragraphs for development. Clearly, every word had to pull the story ahead. I isolated five crucial stages or incidents of the story and assigned one paragraph to each. One paragraph, for example, to show how adventure deepened to love!

Short articles offer excellent training. To make the most of limited space, you have to pay utmost attention to craft. From all the things you could include or want to say you must select ruthlessly those items and only those items that are relevant to your theme. For example, in a 1,000-word article for the *Boston Globe* on the travail of buying clothes in China, I tried to explain why I had to buy summer dresses and skirts, which I hadn't worn for years at home: in June my Chinese male colleagues wore shorts and undershirts to the office, but because of so-called feudal ideas women risked condemnation if they exposed their thighs. Long pants were out of the question because of the torrid heat and lack of air conditioning. But all that gab would have filled one paragraph. Was it absolutely necessary? Reluctantly I admitted that the reader who didn't know me wouldn't wonder why I was desperate to buy dresses in the first place. I left out the whole issue as tangential to my main theme.

Sometimes when constructing an article, you'll find a chunk of material that, no matter what you do, seems to destroy the main flow of the article and yet seems important to pass on to the reader. Try taking it out and making it into a sidebar, a separate item designed to accompany a longer article and often placed on a facing page or amidst the main article in a box. On the other hand, perhaps the overflow deserves to be developed into a separate article, on the same topic but with a different theme and angle.

In Chapter 7 I discuss how to examine focus and style critically when revising an article. Here let me just advise you not to feel bound by all the taboos you learned in school. Feel free to use the word "I" or incomplete sentences, or write paragraphs without a topic sentence—if it works. Look at sample articles in the publications you are aiming at to see what tone and level of informality might be appropriate.

7 / Revising an Article

About ten years ago, soon after I submitted my 230-page dissertation to my graduate school adviser, he wrote back with praise, accepting it and adding, "I have no revisions to suggest." This last part impressed my fellow students tremendously. "No revisions—wow!" they would breathe while I basked in their admiration. Like them, I assumed that not being asked to revise indicated great intelligence. Recently, however, with my 2,000-word article on older women students for *Ms.*, I went through no less than eight drafts. What has happened? Have I become stupid? Far from it. I would be mortified today to see the clumsy, overwritten prose of my thesis in print. No, I have acquired professional standards.

Virtually all professional writers rewrite. Some go so far as to say writing *is* rewriting. For writers who spill out fast first drafts as if through a direct electronic hookup between mind and paper, it's obvious why revisions might help. In a rush, sentences often come out colorless, clumsy, clichéd, repetitious; top-of-the-head arguments may hide logical holes or need substantiating evidence; organization may be jumbled or unclear. But what about writers like me who rarely type a sentence without weighing, rearranging, adjusting? Even so, two aspects of writing for publication dictate an inescapable stage of revision.

First, writing for publication requires that you have made your meaning clear and convincing for an audience, not just for yourself. The best judge of whether you have really said what you intended to say will always be someone other than yourself. Have you failed to explain something obvious to you that will baffle or mislead someone who doesn't know everything you do? Even highly experienced writers used to detaching themselves from their work can't always tell. Also, although all the pieces of your article are unequivocal and appropriate, their overall effect may not be what you intended. One reader of an early draft of my recent *Ms.* article thought I portrayed the older women students as so many self-destructive misfits. Her reaction stunned me, since I had meant to blame the system for trying to force round people into square holes, not the women with more complicated lives than the average eighteen- to twenty-two-year-old. Yet when I looked at the pattern of my quotes, I saw her point. By including such dramatic details as one woman's hair falling out from stress and another having to drink to sleep, I was making them sound like losers who couldn't take the pressure. My friend's feedback helped me focus the article more clearly and eliminate the extreme characterizations that had tilted it contrary to my conscious plan.

Second, except for hard, factual reporting, writing involves interpretation, a kind of brainwork that happens gradually rather than all at once. The process of discovery usually continues throughout the process of writing. That is, while writing you're usually still finding connections, trying to articulate what's implicit and crystallizing the significance of crucial facts and ideas. Thinking you have finished doesn't mean you actually have. Revision offers the chance to keep on digging for nuggets of truth. In draft 4 of my article on older women students, for example, I wrote: "I offered an experience-based course on feminism that de-emphasized grades and my role as an authority, out of assumptions that failed to fit the needs of many women in the course." By draft 6 I realized I had to be more specific and spent hours articulating why I had designed my course as I had and why my assumptions frustrated the older women.

No matter how careful a stylist you are, then, rewriting

improves your chances of producing publishable work that communicates as you would like it to. It's also the time to clean up sloppy craftsmanship. But you need to be able to look at your writing dispassionately, as a stranger might. Time helps. Even letting a draft sit overnight gives you distance on what you've written. Wait a week and poor transitions, dull paragraphs and bad puns will jump out at you as if red ink were already all over the page. Feedback from friends, relatives and especially fellow writers helps too. I've found I get the most fruitful criticism when I provide my friendly critics with specific questions to consider when reading my draft, like, Are there any parts of the article you don't understand? Can you think of anything important I've left out? Anything that could be cut? Does the writing get jumpy anywhere?

BEGIN WITH THE OVERALL STRUCTURE

Ideally, you should scrutinize the larger elements of overall structure and content first, before turning to word-by-word surgery. Here's a checklist to use for your first read-through:

1. *Lead.* Is yours lively and engaging? Or have you mucked around for a few paragraphs first? Editors call this "throat clearing"; lop off the preparatory noise and begin where you're all warmed up.

2. *Body.* Do you deliver on the promise, implicit or explicit, in your lead? Or have you written a substantially different article than the reader would expect from your first few paragraphs? If so, either change your lead or rewrite the rest of the article.

3. *Conclusion.* Is yours fresh and powerful? It should add something—an echo, a humorous or poignant twist, a challenge—instead of just restating what you've already said.

4. *Organization.* Are your paragraphing and sectioning clear enough to keep your reader constantly on track? Don't

worry about providing subheads but do indicate section breaks with asterisks. Consider the possibility of streamlining some passages by arranging information in numbered or bulleted lists (as here).

5. *Length.* If you've overshot your target length, see if a whole paragraph or even a whole section can be sliced off. Even if you're under your limit, check for digressions.

6. *Substantiation.* Have you left any crucial parts uncorroborated or vague? Remember, for every abstract, general statement you should provide specifics, quotes, examples or anecdotes.

7. *Audience.* In focus, tone, level of technicality and scope, have you tailored your article to its intended audience?

And here are some additional "macro" considerations that apply to certain kinds of articles:

Personal experience pieces. Have you included enough background information for the reader to understand the experience's impact on you? Do you recreate the experience step by step for the reader, not with summaries but with language that evokes specific pictures? Teachers and editors call this "showing" rather than "telling." See the *Ms.* article accompanying this chapter for my struggle to "show, not tell," how my romance in China changed me.

Editorials/opinion pieces. Have you stated your thesis, your main point, in one sentence near the beginning? Did you acknowledge the strongest or best-known argument of your opponents and refute it? Don't depend on emotionally loaded language to make your case for you; use a reasonable tone and back up your points with evidence or compelling reasons.

Expository/informational articles. Have you indicated in the text the source of all quotes and statistics and every expert's credentials? For any controversial statement, be sure to signal that it is debatable, preferably by including the opposing view.

How-to articles. Did you define all terms the reader may not know? Did you anticipate and head off possible confusions and misunderstandings, and include safety precautions the reader ought to observe? A fresh introduction and conclusion and sentence variety can do wonders for a piece of this type.

Profiles. Your purpose here is to bring a person to life on the page. Have you woven together quotes, background information and imaginative (though valid) characterizations? Make sure you focus on your subject, not you.

Don't imagine that you're finished! The fine tuning—and, usually, the pruning—comes next. After years of being edited by editors and writer friends and of wrestling with punishing word limits, I've realized that it's always wise to pretend that publication hinges on trimming another 200, 300 or even 400 words from your article. Each time you'll discover new ways to tighten your prose. Strange as this may sound, skillful cutting can add more than it takes away. The goal, after all, is not Calvin Coolidge–like laconism but writing that is coiled like a spring, each part holding tension for the whole.

FINE TUNING

In what follows, I'll try to spell out the ten most valuable lessons I've learned about "micro" editing, the word-by-word surgery. The accompanying articles illustrate some of these points.

1. *Strong verbs.* Change passive verbs to active ones—reword sentences getting by with the verb "to be"—and I guarantee that your sentences will lose flab you may not even have

seen. Strunk and White and most authorities recommend this; it works.

2. *Transitions.* Lisa Collier Cool writes, "I've known writers to spend an hour revising and polishing a *single* sentence in a draft" (emphasis hers). Well, I've been known to spend an hour trying to fix one or two transitions, those devices that stitch sentence to sentence and paragraph to paragraph. Adept transitions account for at least one-third of the grace and coherence of good writing, I'm convinced, so I don't begrudge the time. Most writing manuals cover transitions; Tarshis (see List of Resources, page 125) is particularly good.

3. *Repetition.* If you've glued a piece together with subtle repeats of words, phrases and images, you needn't waste precious space explaining and introducing and reintroducing ideas with topic sentences. Kubis and Howland write, "Vary your words. Use synonyms. Do not use the same word twice in a paragraph (other than 'and,' 'the,' etc.)." Ludicrous advice— just try following it for the preceding paragraph! *Always* repeat a word rather than resort to clumsy substitutes.

4. *Music.* Read your work out loud and edit it for sound and rhythm. Clunky sentences, like mismatched socks, will distract many in your audience.

5. *Emphasis.* Cheney's *Getting the Words Right* taught me that placing a word or idea at the end of a sentence, paragraph or chapter emphasizes it most. The second most emphatic position is the beginning. Put something in the middle and it might as well be entombed. With these simple principles, you can inject drama into the dullest subject.

6. *White space, silence.* From *Hot Water Man,* an obscure British novel by Deborah Moggach, I saw the possibilities of allowing events to happen off the page, not just between chapters but even between paragraphs. Done skillfully, this increases the involvement of the reader, who constructs the

unmentioned in his or her imagination. I called on this technique in my "Falling in Love in China."

7. *Verbal junk.* During revision you must slash away like a samurai at jargon, clichés, empty words (e.g., "lovely"), unnecessary intensifiers (e.g., "really"), surplus images and verbiage. Cheney, Cook and Zinsser (see Resources) show how.

8. *Spelling and grammar.* Ask the sharpest English teacher, editor or writer you know to pinpoint your weaknesses and then case everything you write for that tendency. Only recently, when a literary magazine asked me to rewrite a short story, did I realize that because I wrote by ear I often produced confusing misplaced modifiers. I regularly search for and destroy them now.

9. *Sexism, racism, etc.* Avoid racial, gender, age and other stereotyping. Don't refer to "writers and their wives," contrast "Asian-Americans" with "Americans" or write as if everyone is white unless proven otherwise. For a philosophy guidebook, I wrote at first that careless students had slipped misspelled words into the Smith College computer center's spell-check program; I changed "students" to "users" when my coauthor pointed out that faculty or staff could equally have been the culprits. Remember that as a writer you can challenge common assumptions if you're vigilant yourself.

10. *Scholarly mannerisms.* If you're an academic, you're used to forestalling every possible objection, no matter how obscure. You'll lose a general reader if you do that. Assert. Come out of your don's robes or else stick to professional journals. For general audiences you can use contractions and write "I" instead of "this writer" or "this paper."

One freelance writer I know confessed that when she was starting out an editor asked her for 600 words on a certain subject. "I thought 1,200 words would be twice as good," she laughs now. The editor was not amused. It's up to you to trim your article to requested size, plus or minus 10 percent.

SAMPLE REVISION 1

Based on my query letter, *Ms.* assigned me an article on how my romance in China changed me. The following is the version I submitted after struggling to fit the story into 900 words. I've numbered the paragraphs to make it easier to discuss *Ms.*'s comments and suggestions.

As you read (or after your first reading), notice the piece's structure: paragraph 1 is the lead, paragraph 2 the background, paragraphs 3 through 7 the development and paragraph 8 the conclusion.

CHINA AND THE SINGLE WOMAN [First Version]

[1] Several months into my year of working in China, I drew a photo out of an envelope in the privacy of my hotel apartment and blushed. The picture showed the lover I had left behind and me posing in T-shirts and shorts, with one of my legs lolling across his and his hand casually on my bare thigh. How could I let the maids see that! I thought as I reached for a scissors and snipped off the embarrassing lower portion. It wasn't until after I had propped the doctored photo on my bureau that I stopped to reflect on the strange power of China's pervasive puritanism.

[2] In late 1983, China was a country where women dared not wear shorts in public, where "marriage" was often called on as a euphemism for sexual relations, and where a film's bedroom kiss on the cheek and young couples cycling abreast on dark streets, the man's arm draped around the woman's shoulder, were signs of liberalization. And reality was not much more salacious than appearances, I learned: most urban young adults had no opportunity for sexual experience before marriage, and millions of married couples faithfully endured long separations—two or three full years, or a decade or more in separate provinces, together only one month in twelve.

[3] Very little in Chinese movies, magazines, ad images, conversations, even glances and postures confirmed that sexual needs existed before or beyond the marriage bed. My

reaction to the photo showed that such prudishness could induce prudish behavior, but could the denial tame normal biological urges? Even as I appeared to adapt, my sense of deprivation mounted. "How can you bear it?" I finally burst out one day to a Chinese friend, an athletic, educated, intense man of 24, presumably a virgin. "Waiting is also a kind of happiness," he replied sagely. I shook my head in violent disagreement.

[4] Soon I got to know another man, a tall, talented graduate student, unmarried at 29 because he dreaded a humdrum existence that would foil his ambitions. We shared our life stories and discussed philosophy, politics, families and relationships. "If we were in the United States," I eventually confided, "I would already have tried to seduce you." "Then we're in the wrong country," Zhu brooded. He smoked in silence for a while. "But let's try," he whispered.

[5] What ensued, however, was a courtship much more like a Chinese than an American one. Our first kiss was stolen in an elevator. We schemed, generally in vain, for a way to be alone, undetected. The usual Chinese need to dodge gossip was in our case imperative: in his field, unauthorized contact with foreigners was forbidden. Ordinarily we could do no more than walk and talk, walk and talk in places where we hoped no one who knew him would see us. Often I would go home without even having been able to touch his hand.

[6] Without physical intimacy, we nonetheless deepened our knowledge of one another. He discovered and accepted my impatience and quicksilver changes in mood. I came to admire his resourcefulness and courage while laughing off his tendency to lose things and his aversion to rain. Against my lobbying for taking the risks that might allow us the gratification I craved, Zhu argued caution. "If we're not careful now, we can only do the things once, or twice, or three times," he warned. I realized he was steering us toward a longer goal and fell even more precipitously in love.

[7] Near the end of my year in China, I began to recoil from letters recounting details of the kind of instant affairs I'd once taken for granted. Zhu and I, near-strangers to each

other's bodies, were pondering marriage. Trying for the permission we would need to marry in China was too uncertain, we agreed. And I had a stubborn compunction. I wouldn't marry someone without proof that we were sexually compatible, I told him. "Why?" he scoffed. "That's only ten percent, twenty percent at the most, of a relationship." I just stood for a while looking at him while this wisdom sank in.

[8] Back home, I am plotting for Zhu to join me in the United States. Our American movies, magazines, ad images and some looks I get in the street try to convince me to give up or at least have a fling in the meantime. But two things I learned in China are still with me: sex needn't be the glue of love and commitment, and waiting can also bring happiness.

The *Ms.* editors objected to paragraphs 6 and 7: too much "telling" and not enough "showing." I leaped from the circumstances to their effect on me without demonstrating why I became able to accept what had been an intolerable situation. I asked the reader to take my word for it that I changed my attitude instead of exhibiting the change on the page. Hence the conclusion wasn't believable. The piece needed more feeling, the editors advised; I had to do a better job of setting the reader up for my falling in love.

Their comments provoked frantic canvassing of my memories. Why *had* adventure deepened to love? What incidents encapsulated that metamorphosis? Why had Zhu's "once, or twice or three times" and "ten percent, twenty percent" remarks impressed me so profoundly? And what in the world could I drop from the original version to make room for more development?

As you'll see in the following final version that appeared in *Ms.*, I dropped just a few sentences and phrases from paragraphs 5, 6, 7 and 8. I expanded paragraph 6 into two paragraphs, showing the progress of our romance with a new incident and its aftermath. I explained more specifically why Zhu's remarks impressed me.

Notice also that the final version gains power through repetition and more dramatic transitions. In addition to repeating "shorts" in paragraphs 1 and 2, and "waiting" in paragraph 3 and the last sentence, I repeated "flush" in the two paragraphs that expanded original paragraph 6 and "strange power" in the lead and conclusion. And in the new version every paragraph ending provides space for readers' imaginations to react to the implicit significance of the narrated events.

The editors accepted the slightly longer new version. Here's how the article appeared in the February 1986 *Ms.* And by the way, Reader, I married him.

FALLING IN LOVE IN CHINA

[1] Several months into my year of working in China, I drew a photo out of an envelope in the privacy of my hotel apartment and blushed. The picture showed the lover I had left behind and me posing in T-shirts and shorts, with one of my legs lolling across his and his hand casually on my bare thigh. How could I let the maids see that! I thought as I reached for a scissors and snipped off the embarrassing lower portion. It wasn't until after I had propped the doctored photo on my bureau that I stopped to reflect on the strange power of China's pervasive puritanism.

[2] In late 1983, China was a country where women dared not wear shorts in public, where "marriage" was often used as a euphemism for sexual relations, and where a film's bedroom kiss on the cheek and young couples cycling abreast on dark streets, the man's arm draped around the woman's shoulder, were signs of liberalization. And reality was not much more salacious than appearances, I learned: most urban young adults had no opportunity for sexual experience before marriage, and millions of married couples faithfully endured long separations—two or three full years, or a decade or more in separate provinces, together one month in 12.

[3] Very little in Chinese movies, magazines, ad images, conversations, even glances and postures confirmed that sexual needs existed before or beyond the marriage bed. My reaction to the photo showed that such prudishness could

induce prudish behavior, but could the denial tame normal biological urges? Even as I appeared to adapt, my sense of deprivation mounted. "How can you bear it?" I finally burst out one day to a Chinese friend, an athletic, educated, intense man of 24, presumably a virgin. "Waiting is also a kind of happiness," he replied sagely. I shook my head in violent disagreement.

[4] Soon I got to know another man, a tall, talented graduate student, unmarried at 29 because he dreaded a humdrum existence that would foil his ambitions. We shared our life stories and discussed philosophy, politics, families, and relationships. "If we were in the United States," I eventually confided, "I would already have tried to seduce you." "Then we're in the wrong country," Zhu brooded. He smoked in silence for a while. "But let's try," he whispered.

[5] What ensued, however, was a courtship much more like a Chinese than an American one. We schemed, generally in vain, for a way to be alone, undetected. Ordinarily we could do no more than walk and talk, walk and talk in places where we hoped no one who knew him would see us. The usual Chinese need to dodge gossip was in our case imperative: in his field, unauthorized contact with foreigners was forbidden. Often I would go home without even having been able to touch his hand.

[6a] Yet as our meetings continued, he discovered and accepted my impatience and quicksilver changes in mood. I came to admire his resourcefulness and courage while laughing off his aversion to rain. "What is love? Do you think love can last forever?" became a more frequent topic of conversation. One night, after I walked him past a hotel guard who might have challenged him, Zhu turned to me with an exalted flush on his face. "My heart is pounding," he confessed. "You mean because of the guard?" "Not entirely," he replied. Then, still wearing that peculiar look, he nudged me into the shadows, touched his lips quietly to mine, and walked quickly away from the guard and me toward the bus stop.

[6b] If I thought taking that risk signaled a determination to have an affair no matter what the dangers, I was wrong. The

Chinese script for romance ran otherwise. "If we're not careful now, we can only do the things once, or twice, or three times," Zhu later explained. It was my turn to flush and get flustered. I realized he was steering us toward a longer goal, one that scared me but also excited me, and the spell grew.

[7] Zhu and I, near-strangers to each other's bodies, began pondering marriage. Trying for the permission we would need to marry in China was too uncertain, we agreed. And I had a stubborn compunction. I wouldn't marry someone without proof that we were sexually compatible, I told him. "Why?" he scoffed. "That's only ten percent, twenty percent at the most, of a relationship." As I stood taking this in, it dawned on me that the Chinese way, where 80 or 90 percent was loyalty, affection, and mutual respect, was what I had always wanted.

[8] Back home, I am plotting for Zhu to join me in the United States. Our American movies, magazines, ad images, and some looks I get in the street have strangely little power to persuade me to have a fling in the meantime. Two things I learned in China keep company with me: sex needn't be the glue of love and waiting can also bring happiness.

SAMPLE REVISION 2

I've included the submitted and published versions of this article because *The Progressive*'s skillful editing drove home to me for the first time how cluttered and overloaded with modifiers my prose was. *Progressive* editors slashed excessive examples, redundancies, unnecessary explanations and trimmed sentences that were simply too long and complex. Their revision illustrates many of the "micro" principles listed earlier. I think the two versions are worth studying in detail, to see how editing made my article much more readable.

When I received the prepublication computer printout of the article, I found three small errors and objected to their rewrite of my last sentence. For my "It will be interesting to

see" they substituted "I have my doubts." That was too negative, I explained. Couldn't we go back to my original ending?
No, the article needed to end with more punch, the editor
argued. After much discussion we thought up "It will be a stiff
challenge," which satisfied us both. The article appeared in the
June 1985 *Progressive*.

[*Submitted Version*]

CHINA: MAY YOU BECOME RICH

[1] Last year, as the biting winds of late January blew
through the battened windows of Beijing's Foreign Languages
Press, where I was working, the chilly halls often rang with
reckless hilarity. Like a Santa Claus spreading holiday mirth,
Zhao Yihe, our slightly tubby Deputy Chief Editor, would
divert people going about their business with the salute of the
season: "Gongxi facai!"—may you become rich!—uttered
with clasped hands upraised and shaken from side to side of
his grinning head. He never failed to win a highspirited return
of the Spring Festival greeting from the person so hailed and
chuckles from everyone within earshot.

[2] This was the first year in decades that the traditional
wish of prosperity for the new year had been ventured in
China's capital, someone explained to me, which made sense
of the atmosphere of childish delight and unjaded pleasure he
seemed to evoke even among the sourest grownups. Undoubt-
edly hearing the greeting burst from a dedicated Party member
and leader added a piquant dash of irony to the nostalgia that
made his older coworkers laugh. I chalked the affair up to
Zhao Yihe's instinct for being in the progressive vanguard.
Late in 1983 he had strutted around the office in a Western
suit and tie, declaring "This is not cultural pollution," a month
before Hu Yaobang, chairman of the Chinese Communist
Party, had proclaimed much the same thing.

[3] As with the Western clothes, only someone familiar
with China's history could fathom why wealth should be an
issue at all. Throughout the reign of Mao, creature comforts
and conveniences, not to mention luxuries, loomed unimpor-

tant beside the paramount goal of revolution through class struggle and the drive to build a society founded on social equality and cooperation. Now Deng Xiaoping's regime derides that ideal of equality as in effect no more than a way of keeping the people equally poor and China backward. The new theory, buttressed mainly by metaphors and examples, is that when people are encouraged to become as rich as possible, those who become rich first will spur on the laggards, who will soon catch up instead of becoming yet more impoverished.

[4] By and large American observers have applauded the turnaround and seized on the signs that China is hurtling toward a consumer society like ours—the jeans, cosmetic surgery, even private cars and trucks that have appeared or reappeared on the scene. It is harder for us to recognize the phenomena that contravene our own cultural myths. Yet between the Chinese New Year of 1984 and my departure from China in the fall, I learned much to convince me that the picture of the Chinese marching joyfully, finally, and unanimously toward a rich future is much too simple. Despite the Horatio Alger tone of the "enterprising peasant rakes in his first hundred thousand" stories in the Chinese media and the eager, increasingly discerning customers always mobbing Beijing's most famous stores, I picked up numerous indications in everyday events at the Press and in my research for a book on the resurgence of private business in China's cities that the government's new legitimation of wealth is meeting a complicated reception.

[5] One of my officemates, a youngish Party member who seemed to have a dual personality of jokester and workhorse, had a habit of turning to me with gnomic remarks when we were alone. One of these, occasioned either by the street's "free market" that floated a cacophony of quacking and crowing, bicycle bells and general hubbub up to our windows or by the news that I was going to investigate China's private business for the Press, or perhaps both, was: "China is not like some other countries. Here making money is not the most important thing." I knew that he didn't mean to convey contempt for money and the better food, clothes and stereo ca-

sette tape players it could now buy. Almost everyone in our section moonlighted translating English into Chinese or vice versa for extra cash. I knew too that if the government raised my colleagues' salaries to equal or surpass factory workers', as Deng Xiaoping had urged, none of them would refuse. But it took me a while to catch on to the pervasive prejudice remaining against people who step too quickly or too far along the moneymaking road.

[6] When I began interviewing private businesspeople in Beijing, Tianjin and several provincial capitals, I had no trouble getting many older, recidivist (so to speak) private operators to detail the persecutions and humiliations they had suffered during the Cultural Revolution and even earlier for activities that to Maoists smacked of capitalism. Hu Dapeng, for example, a 51-year-old Beijing man with an intense manner, began to repair radios and TVs privately after he lost his regular job at a radio factory during the economically hard period of 1960–62. With the outbreak of the Cultural Revolution, his only source of income disappeared and his social status plummeted from second-class citizen to a dreg of society. When he repaired appliances secretly to make some money, he was accused of running an "underground factory," and when he didn't he was excoriated anyway for having been a "tail of capitalism." "Even my children were looked down on," he told me. "I had almost no hope."

[7] After the Party's official shift of priorities in December 1978 from class struggle to the "four modernizations" program, people like Hu could return to their old occupations, some more lucratively than ever. When I asked him if he was discriminated against now, he became even more serious and earnest. "Now the country encourages people to get wealthy through correct and reasonable means," he explained. "In the past people thought poverty was glorious and wealth sinful. Before, I wouldn't have dared buy a refrigerator even if I had the money. The leaders would have condemned me as a 'millionaire.' I bought my motorcycle in 1981, but I didn't dare ride it in public. I worried that the officials would get 'red eyes' [be jealous]. I was afraid that the policy would change. But

now I dare ride my motorcycle even to political meetings. I can make a lot of money and no one will say anything against me now."

[8] Yet the picture that finally emerged was of the courage or desperation that it took for city people to work outside the auspices of the state. "Why shouldn't I be a pacesetter?" argued Peng Mingyin, a bulky private meat dealer who bragged that he was the number-one taxpayer in Jinan. "Many people tell me not to expand my business because bigger trees attract more wind and because it's dangerous for a pig to become too strong. But only by more people doing this kind of thing will China become a powerful country in the world." An equally spirited young clothes peddler in Henan province burst out in answer to one of my questions, "Of course I'd rather have a regular state job, even if I made less money. This isn't steady," and then turned to my interpreter, "Uh-oh, is it okay for me to say that?" In Beijing, a young man repairing bicycles with his father openly carried a grudge against the repair shop that had forced him to quit his job because of his allergy to oil. "Working here, people say nasty things to my face," he complained. "As an individual businessperson, I can find a girlfriend but not a very good one. My father doesn't care about this because he's too old." And perhaps the finest private tailor in Tianjin, herself long married, confirmed that the fear of prejudice kept many single people away from private business. "Many young people have this kind of burden," Gao Zhixin declared.

[9] Indeed, a close look at the range of people actually engaged in private business revealed that in many areas, the bulk of private businesspeople consisted of formerly jobless people over 35—people no longer eligible, by and large, for state employment. To Beijing University sociologist Yuan Fang, the figures showed that the government's strenuous propaganda campaigns about the glory of getting rich through individual enterprise were not having their intended effect. "Restoring private business was supposed to provide another channel of employment for youth," he told me. "But almost all job-waiting youth don't want to do it."

[10] Besides the greater security of state employment, I believe that the explanation must include not only a rational fear of setting oneself up for trouble when political winds change, but also a pervasive distaste for obvious moneygrubbing. During watermelon season, I learned that one woman and her teenaged children selling small mountains of the fruit in front of our office were the family of a worker in our bureau. They had reportedly already made a small fortune, enough to consider buying a truck. When I asked colleagues if they envied them, the answers were equivocal. But when I asked if they respected them, the response was uniformly "no." I suspect that if asked to defend themselves, the peddler family would adopt a defensive tone like that of this *China Youth Daily* article intended to praise a young inventor/entrepreneur: "With his solar heating project completed, he is planning to expand his business with several assistants. From now on, each year's profit, if not ten or twenty yuan, will be one hundred or several hundred thousands. And what of it? The labor commission approves."

[11] The current line is that only when income is pegged to effort and concrete results can people's initiative and enthusiasm be fully unleashed. Yet one colleague told me that before my arrival in China, our unit had voted down an incentive system because the idea of making the others look bad by trying one's hardest made many of them uncomfortable. In fact, even without an incentive system, capable people who appeared too ambitious were looked at askance. The bonus system in place in 1984 tended to penalize individuals for poor attendance and reward the group for the quantity of work it produced. An observation made by several Chinese who had studied in the United States sums up the major obstacle to the success of an incentive system in China's bureaucracies: "In the United States everyone tries to be different. In China everyone wants to be the same." That tendency will be a powerful hindrance to the urban reforms the Communist Party has pledged to institute beginning in 1985.

[12] Assuming that the problem of assigning a cash value to the quality as well as quantity of translation, editing and

book production could be solved, those reforms would invite a kind of conflict and competition that has been very muted into the office and that very well might add nervous or even sarcastic edges to exchanges of wishes for prosperity. One boss, when I came to him frustrated because a staffer in another part of the bureau seemed to be reluctant to perform a task within his duties for me, made this sardonic remark: "Offer him some extra money and I guarantee he'll do his job." I can't imagine many of the Chinese people I knew well becoming enthusiastic exponents of the philosophy of "Time is money and efficiency is life," as the most advanced cronies of Deng Xiaoping like to put it. Many of my colleagues were too sensible for that. "Don't work too hard," Zhao Yihe and others, for example, would often admonish me. "Don't ruin your health." Can the modernizationists now ruling China continue to glorify wealth without fostering greed, selfishness, divisiveness and dissension? It will be interesting to see.

[Published Version]

THE CHINA SYNDROME: POTHOLES ON THE CAPITALIST ROAD

[1] As the biting winds of late January blew through the battened windows of Beijing's Foreign Languages Press, where I worked last year, the chilly halls often rang with reckless hilarity. Like a Santa Claus spreading holiday mirth, Zhao Yihe, our slightly tubby deputy chief editor, would divert people going about their business with the salute of the season, *Gongxi facai,* "may you become rich," uttered with clasped hands upraised and shaken from side to side of his grinning head. He never failed to win a high-spirited response from the person so hailed and chuckles from everyone within earshot.

[2] This was the first time in decades that the traditional wish of prosperity for the new year had been voiced in China's capital, and it evoked an atmosphere of unjaded pleasure. Hearing the greeting from a dedicated Communist Party leader added a dash of irony to the nostalgia. I chalked the affair up to Zhao Yihe's instinct for being in the vanguard.

Late in 1983, he had strutted around the office in a Western suit and tie, declaring, "This is *not* cultural pollution." A month later, Hu Yaobang, chairman of the Chinese Communist Party, proclaimed much the same thing.

[3] Throughout Mao Zedong's reign, creature comforts and conveniences, not to mention luxuries, took a back seat. The paramount goal was revolution through class struggle and construction of a society founded on social equality and cooperation. Now Deng Xiaoping's regime derides the ideal of equality and dismisses it as a way of keeping the people equally poor and China backward. The new theory is that when people are encouraged to become rich, those who get there first will spur the laggards to catch up.

[4] Most American observers have applauded the abundant signs that China is hurtling toward a consumer society—the jeans, cosmetic surgery, even private cars and trucks that have appeared or reappeared. But between the Chinese New Year of 1984 and my departure from China in the fall, I saw much that raised doubts about the new image of the Chinese marching in joyous lockstep toward a rich future. Despite the Horatio Alger tone of the "enterprising peasant rakes in his first hundred thousand" stories in the Chinese media, despite the eager, increasingly discerning buyers who mob Beijing's most famous stores, I picked up many indications that the government's legitimation of wealth is meeting a complicated and ambiguous reception.

[5] One of my co-workers, a hard-working young party member, had a habit of turning to me with cryptic remarks when we were alone. One of these was, "China is not like some other countries. Here making money is not the most important thing." I knew he didn't mean to convey contempt for money and the better food, clothes, and stereo tape players it could now buy. Almost everyone in our section earned extra cash by moonlighting as a translator of English into Chinese or vice versa. I knew, too, that if the government raised my colleagues' salaries to equal or surpass factory workers', as Deng Xiaoping had urged, none of them would refuse. But it took me a while to realize there was still a pervasive prejudice against people

who stepped too quickly or too far along the moneymaking road.

[6] When I began interviewing operators of private businesses in Beijing, Tianjin, and several provincial capitals, older operators were quick to detail the persecutions and humiliations they had suffered during the Cultural Revolution. Hu Dapeng, a fifty-one-year-old Beijing man, began repairing radios and television sets privately after he lost his regular job at a radio factory during the hard times of 1960–1962. With the outbreak of the Cultural Revolution, his only source of income disappeared and his social status plummeted; instead of a second-class citizen, he was a virtual untouchable. When he repaired appliances secretly to earn some money, he was accused of running an "underground factory," and when he didn't he was still excoriated as a "tail of capitalism." "Even my children were looked down on," he told me. "I had almost no hope."

[7] After the Party's official shift in December 1978 from class struggle to the "four modernizations" program, people like Hu could return to their old occupations. When I asked him if he is discriminated against today, he said, "Now the country encourages people to get wealthy through correct and reasonable means. In the past, people thought poverty was glorious and wealth sinful. Before, I wouldn't have dared buy a refrigerator even if I had the money. The leaders would have condemned me as a 'millionaire.' I bought my motorcycle in 1981, but I didn't dare ride it in public. I worried that the officials would get 'red eyes' [be jealous]. I was afraid that the policy would change. But now I dare ride my motorcycle even to political meetings. I can make a lot of money and no one will say anything against me now."

[8a] Yet it became clear to me that it often took courage or desperation for city people to work outside the auspices of the State. "Why shouldn't I be a pacesetter?" argued Peng Mingyin, a private meat dealer who boasted that he was the number-one taxpayer in Jinan. "Many people tell me not to expand my business because bigger trees attract more wind and because it's dangerous for a pig to become too strong. But

only by more people doing this kind of thing will China become a powerful country in the world."

[8b] An equally spirited young clothes peddler in Henan province burst out in answer to one of my questions, "Of course I'd rather have a regular state job, even if I made less money. This isn't steady." Then he turned to my interpreter and asked, "Is it okay for me to say that?" In Beijing, a young man repairing bicycles carried a grudge against the repair shop that had forced him to quit his job because of his allergy to oil. "Working here, people say nasty things to my face," he complained. "As an individual businessperson, I can find a girlfriend but not a very good one." And a private tailor in Tianjin, herself long married, confirmed that the fear of prejudice kept many single people away from private business. "Many young people have this kind of burden," Gao Zhixin said.

[9] In many areas, most of the people in private business are formerly jobless individuals who have passed the age of thirty-five and are no longer eligible, by and large, for state employment. To Beijing University sociologist Yuan Fang, the figures show that the government's strenuous propaganda campaigns about the glory of getting rich through individual enterprise are not having their intended effect. "Restoring private business was supposed to provide another channel of employment for youth," he told me. "But almost all job-waiting youth don't want to do it."

[10] Besides the greater security of state employment, the explanation must include a rational fear of setting oneself up for trouble when political winds change, as well as a pervasive distaste for obvious moneygrubbing. During watermelon season, I learned that one woman and her teen-aged children selling mountains of the fruit in front of our office were the family of a worker in our bureau. They had reportedly already made a small fortune, enough to consider buying a truck. When I asked colleagues whether they envied them, the answers were equivocal. But when I asked whether they respected them, the response was uniformly "no." I suspect that if asked to defend themselves, the peddler family would adopt

a defensive tone like that of this *China Youth Daily* article intended to praise a young inventor/entrepreneur: "With his solar heating project completed, he is planning to expand his business with several assistants. From now on, each year's profit, if not ten or twenty yuan, will be one hundred or several hundred thousands. And what of it? The labor commission approves."

[11a] The current line holds that only when income is pegged to effort and results can individual initiative and enthusiasm be fully unleashed. But one colleague told me that before I arrived in China, our unit had voted down an incentive system because many disliked the idea of making the others look bad by trying one's hardest. In fact, capable people who appeared too ambitious were looked at askance. The bonus system in place in 1984 tended to penalize individuals for poor attendance and reward the group for the quantity of work it produced.

[11b] An observation made by several Chinese who had studied in the United States sums up the major obstacle to the success of an incentive system in China's bureaucracies: "In the United States, everyone tries to be different. In China everyone wants to be the same." That tendency will be a powerful hindrance to the urban reforms the Communist Party has pledged to institute beginning this year.

[12] I can't imagine many of the Chinese people I knew well becoming enthusiastic exponents of the philosophy of "Time is money and efficiency is life," as the most advanced cronies of Deng Xiaoping like to put it. My colleagues were too sensible for that. "Don't work too hard," Zhao Yihe and others would often admonish me. "Don't ruin your health." Can the modernizationists now ruling China continue to glorify wealth without fostering greed, selfishness, divisiveness, and dissension? It will be a stiff challenge.

8 / Maintaining Credibility

At the Bread Loaf Writers Conference in 1979, John Irving told a story about watching a woman across an airplane aisle read his *World According to Garp*. "She was very absorbed in it," he said, "but suddenly she slammed the book closed and stuffed it into her air-sickness bag. My son was trying to get the woman's attention, pointing to me and indicating, 'He did it! Here he is!' while I tried to sink through my seat. I had done something to break the spell for her. Somewhere in the book I had failed to maintain the fictional dream world, and it was too late to do anything about it."

Nonfiction writers face similar pitfalls. Whether you are writing a query, a cover letter or an article, you must avoid any kind of slip that would make an editor or reader throw down your piece in disgust and complain, "This person doesn't know what he is talking about." I've had that experience as a reader. Once I looked through a new Israeli magazine with an article about "birds of pray"; when I realized the "pray" was not a graceful pun but a misspelling, I felt cheated. Unfortunately, I've provoked that reaction as a writer too. When I submitted a version of my article on nannies to *MD,* editor A. J. Vogl wrote back, "Sorry, this is not for us. Incidentally, not even the most English of English nannies would wear a bowler hat." Obviously I'd incorrectly named the hat I'd seen in pictures of English nanny uniforms. Vogl had probably stopped reading right there, on page 2.

Something as small as one garbled word can have this effect.

While everyone understands that typos steal by the most diligent proofreader, certain kinds of misspellings demolish a person's aura of authority. Once I received an announcement of a doctor launching a practice in "North Hampton," the city in western Massachusetts that should be spelled "Northampton." Would you trust a surgeon who couldn't be bothered with the correct spelling of his new town to cut you open and get every detail of the operation right? I wouldn't. And for a writer to botch *p*'s and *q*'s is even more damning. If you received a query offering an exposé of nefarious leadership in a South American country spelled "Columbia," would you assign the article? Or suppose a writer proposed to interview "the burocrats effected by the new regulations"?

I can suggest three strategies to eliminate these calamitous gaffes. First, when interviewing, always check the spelling of people's names and unfamiliar terms. Even if you hear "John Smith," ask, "Spelled the obvious way?" It could be "Johan Smyth." Or wait till the end of the interview and ask about correct spellings then. If you forget, call your interview subjects back to check before you send in the article. When I wrote a profile of a gardener, she was happy to help me check all the Latin and common flower names in her botany books. Second, you should own at least one good dictionary, an atlas with a good index and a usage handbook; consult them often. If you're not even aware of sticklers' distinctions between *farther* and *further, anxious* and *eager, nauseated* and *nauseous,* study lists of commonly misused words in Cheney, Strunk and White or Venolia (see Resources). Third, proofread meticulously. Don't rely on a spell-check program or a quick read-through to catch all your mistakes. Point to every word with your finger as you read or read aloud slowly to detect the errors.

Dates, figures and people's titles also deserve extra care. No matter how small the lapse, chances are that someone somewhere will notice. For that reason, among others, some magazines employ fact-checkers, professional nitpickers who spend their working days chasing down proof that every detail about to appear in the magazine is accurate. (See Jay McInerny's *Bright Lights, Big City* for a satirical view of the fact-checking department of a publication very like *The New Yorker*.) But most magazines cannot afford such insurance; they rely on writers to be punctilious. Don't let them down. The consequences can be much more serious than a no-thanks letter from an editor. With my second published article for pay, I narrowly escaped ruin in this regard.

My article, published in *The Progressive*, criticized a slew of self-styled experts who argued that adult-child incest was okay. I hadn't researched pornographic magazines myself, but relied on reports from people who had. I wrote, "In 1977, *Screw* magazine offered $200 for girl models; dozens of parents responded." When *The Progressive*'s editor-in-chief called and told me the lawyer for *Screw* magazine had called him and charged that the claim was untrue, I wasn't concerned. I told him to hang on, ran to my desk and found my source and read it to him over the telephone. "But wait," he interrupted. "That says 'an ad in *Screw* magazine,' not '*Screw* magazine.'" I saw the distinction now and suddenly lost my voice. Images of a humiliating court session and a million-dollar judgment were bringing on panic. "I don't think they'll sue," the editor said after a long pause. "I'll offer them an apology and a retraction and get back to you." A smartly worded note in a later issue of the magazine settled the affair.

My mistake didn't turn *The Progressive* against me forever. Four years later it accepted another article from me. But I wouldn't recommend that terrible scare. Be vigilant for any claims that might activate the talents of lawyers. Besides libel, you ought to guard against plagiarism, invasion of privacy, defamation and invention of facts in nonfiction articles.

While I'm not a lawyer, I've read or heard about enough foul-ups by writers to suggest a few steps to take to avoid antagonizing editors or, worse, people and corporations that can afford top attorneys.

• Prevent unintentional plagiarism by rigorously distinguishing in your notes between exact quotes from written sources and summaries in your own words. Few magazines and no newspapers print footnotes, so indicate in the text where you've used other people's ideas. ("As Woody Allen wrote . . ." "According to MIT professor Noam Chomsky . . .")

• Don't confuse investigative reporting and spying. Publishing information that you gathered under false pretenses or while trespassing can land you in hot water. Read DuBoff or Henderson (see Resources) before you act out your journalist-in-a-trenchcoat fantasies.

• If you hire a research assistant, remember that you're still legally and morally responsible for material that appears under your by-line. I think this might keep me doing it all myself even if I could afford to farm out interviews or research.

• When providing photos to accompany an article, secure signed "model releases" from any identifiable person in the photos. Abrams, Henderson and Zobel (see Resources) explain how.

• If you're inclined to provide fake names for your sources in an article, or to construct a composite character, present your case to the editor and let him or her decide. Some magazines routinely use changed names, while many newspapers, especially since Janet Cooke of the *Washington Post* lost a Pulitzer Prize for fabricating sources, won't.

• To settle questions about the accuracy of your reporting, keep your notes and tapes for at least a year after the article you based on them appears.

• Some editors object strongly to writers "plagiarizing themselves." If you've previously published ideas or information anywhere, give your new editor the details, even if you've kept rights (see Chapter 9) to the material.

The issue of credibility can arise even before an article gets written. A number of years ago, I received a call from the editor of a magazine for society ladies, who wanted me to interview a retired diplomat about his sister's involvement in their organization. Another editor I'd written for had recommended me. For only 1,000 words, I would get $500 plus airfare, which struck me as a good deal. Over the next few weeks the editor sent me copies of her magazine, a contract and a plane ticket. She mentioned that she and an associate from the organization would also fly several hundred miles to accompany me to the interview. This seemed odd to me, as if the man we'd be talking with were a foreign head of state. But when we were talking about arrangements for our meeting, I didn't take this oddity into account.

"How will I find you at the airport?" I asked the editor. She described a place to meet and asked me to describe myself. "I look a lot younger than my age, which is thirty," I began. She laughed and replied, "I look just about my age and I don't like to say what that is." "I have brown hair and blue eyes and I'm five foot six," I added, "and I'll be wearing white pants." There was a distinct chill at the other end of the line at this. "Mr. ——— is quite elderly and traditional, you know; you'd better wear a suit," the editor said. At my end I rolled my eyes; I intended to be neat and presentable, but didn't own a "dress-for-success" outfit. Surely Mr. ——— was used to informally dressed journalists! To the editor I was noncommittal. The next day I found a message on my machine informing me that Mr. ——— was ill and that the trip was canceled.

Perhaps Mr. ——— *had* taken ill, but that wasn't the lesson I took away from the fiasco. I saw that I had failed to maintain my credibility. Because I had never reinforced the first editor's recommendation with my résumé, other references or samples of my work, the second editor could well have had last-minute jitters: Here's an unsophisticated young jerk who would waste the precious privilege of an interview with Mr. ——— and make the society ladies look foolish. Since then, whenever an out-of-the-ordinary opportunity pops up, I blitz the editor or client with evidence of my professionalism. I send a résumé, clips and names and phone numbers of people who can vouch for the quality of my work. The general principle here is the same as that underlying earlier examples in this chapter: don't allow doubts a foothold. Be professional and you will be able to get—and keep—assignments.

9 / Rights and Other Technicalities

Tina Timmid, a middle-aged schoolteacher from North Greenwood, Vermont, had had three articles published locally when *Woman's Monthly* replied to her query on her struggle with arthritis: "We'd like to see it." Three exhausting weeks later, Tina sent in the tightest, most dramatic piece she'd ever written. Still, when *Woman's Monthly* accepted the article she was stunned. She signed their contract in a state of shock. When the article appeared, there was a pleasant flurry of excitement in her town, and henceforth North Greenwood referred to her as "Tina the writer."

Two years later, Tina was struggling with an outbreak of writer's block when she read an announcement in her newspaper about an upcoming TV movie in which a Vermont schoolteacher suffering from a potentially crippling case of arthritis is cured through exercises devised by a handsome, troubled veteran who had been a medic in Vietnam. Tina scratched her head and called Burton Broomsby, her second cousin and a lawyer in Boston, who listened, investigated and then called her back. "Tina," he said, "it's a million-dollar production spicing up your article in *Woman's Monthly* with adultery. They can do that legally without your permission and without paying you a dime—you signed away your rights! You were smart enough to write the damned thing, so how the devil could you be so dumb?"

Tina does not exist, but her situation is not as farfetched as it might seem. *Urban Cowboy* and *Perfect,* among other contemporary feature films, originated in nonfiction articles. I don't know whether or not the original authors were frozen out of the films, but they could have been if, like Tina, they'd signed away "all rights." For any article at all, it's important to understand rights terminology and to do so sooner rather than later. In Tina's case, later was too late.

Under the 1978 U.S. copyright law, as soon as you, a freelancer, create any literary work—a poem, article, story or whatever—you hold the copyright. That is, unless and until you give express permission, the work belongs to you and no one else may publish, reprint or adapt it. This protection applies regardless of whether or not you write "Copyright 19xx by Joe Author" on your manuscript and whether or not you officially register the work with the Library of Congress. Although you may not sue for unauthorized use of your work unless you have so registered it, copyright infringement cases are relatively rare and usually get settled by an exchange of letters or phone calls. On the other hand, every sale of every to-be-published item involves a transfer of certain rights you, as creator of the work, originally own. Which rights? You must know the technicalities and stay on your toes.

STANDARD CATEGORIES OF RIGHTS

The following are the most important standard categories of rights for publishing in newspapers and magazines.

First serial rights. Usually magazines buy first serial rights. "Serial" here means "periodical," and "first" implies strict priority of publication. In other words, if you sell first serial rights to a magazine, no one can print that article elsewhere until after the magazine publishes it. Selling first serial rights becomes problematic only when the purchased piece doesn't get published within a reasonable amount of time. If you've sold first serial rights to an article and you get itchy after one or two years pass without publication, all you can do is ask for the return of the rights you sold. If the magazine paid a substantial sum for those rights, however, it will most likely require you to *buy back* the rights. Thus a clause like this in each agreement to sell first rights would be to your advantage: "If [the magazine] does not publish the article within one year of purchase, rights revert to the author, who will not be required to return the purchase price." Unfortunately, many magazines would reject such a clause.

Second serial (or reprint) rights. If your article has appeared or will soon definitely appear in a publication that has purchased first serial rights, you are free to sell second serial or reprint rights to another publication. But you should still inform all subsequent prospective buyers where and when the article has (or will have) already been published. Some magazines and newspapers never reprint articles that have already been published, no matter how obscure the original publication, while others frequently buy reprint rights to articles most of their readers probably didn't see. Check *Writer's Market* for outlets' receptivity to reprints.

One-time rights. The phrase "one-time rights" may come up when a publication wants to reprint an article; also, a newspaper may buy one-time rights to an unpublished article, specifying that the author should not offer it to another newspaper in its circulation area. Buying one-time rights means acquiring the right to publish the article once, irrespective of priority. Theoretically, you could sell one-time rights to one publication and then first rights to another—if you could count on the one-time purchaser holding off publication long enough for the first-rights purchaser to have priority. But generally you should reserve publications that like to buy one-time rights for reprint sales; aim first for those that demand first rights.

All rights. "All rights" is a much more sinister bargain than you might think. The "all" in the phrase indeed means *all:* the right to use it as the basis of a film, to translate and publish it in other languages, to include it on a cassette recording or an electronic information network and to reprint, adapt or resell it anywhere and as many times as the traffic will bear. When you sell all rights you don't even retain the right to use a substantial portion of "your own" material in a book you later write. I put "your own" in quotes because though your name may be on it, in no other sense will your work still be yours (except that you can reclaim the rights to it after thirty-five years). You should do your damnedest to avoid this kind of sale. Many publications that routinely demand all rights get away with it because writers acquiesce. Tell or write the editor, "I'm sorry, but I don't sell all rights." If that doesn't work, then at least make sure they pay you more for all rights than a comparable market pays for first serial rights. As I explain later in this chapter, many editors do negotiate when approached politely and professionally.

Work for hire. If "all rights" hurts freelancers, "work for hire" exploits them. Our copyright law includes an exception for works created as part of an employee's regular employment. In such cases—for example, if your company assigned you the task of writing a guidebook or technical manual, on company time for the benefit of the company—the company, not you, is considered the author and owner of the work. For works created during regular employment, the "work-for-hire" exception is reasonable. But some publications require freelancers to sign a "work-for-hire" clause transferring ownership of the work. That way the publication gets all the advantages of employing an in-house writer without having to pay salary, unemployment insurance, social security and so on. You can never reclaim the rights, and the company could even publish your work under someone else's by-line.

Under no circumstances should you acquiesce to a "work-for-hire" clause. Each time a writer does, he undermines the dignity of the profession and helps perpetuate poor working conditions for writers in general.

Other rights. "First rights" are often qualified with a geographical or language adjective. For example, "first North American (serial) rights," "first U.S. rights," "first English-language rights"; these are self-explanatory. There is no standard, limited set of possibilities—you can always make up a new combination, such as "first Hongkong-Macao rights" or "first South American Portuguese rights." There's also "book rights," the right to publish the article in a book. "Dramatic rights" would mean the right to dramatize the article in a film, TV show or play. I've also seen "non-exclusive anthology rights," which means the right, though not the exclusive right, to republish the piece in an anthology. If a contract includes some other right you don't understand, ask for clarification. And remember that any rights you don't explicitly sign away still belong to you.

Not every publication routinely uses written contracts (or "letters of agreement") to set out explicitly what it is commissioning or buying, the price and other terms of the deal. Keep in mind that while a verbal agreement is still legally considered a contract, it is harder to enforce, for obvious reasons. If an editor calls you to assign or accept an article and doesn't follow up with a signed contract or letter reiterating the terms of the offer, then you should draft a letter outlining the terms of the agreement as you understand them. Enclose a self-addressed stamped envelope for the editor's reply, and you will have an enforceable contract. You can see in the sample assignment confirmation (page 87) how I once worded such a letter.

Not only do contracts, even simple confirmation letters, help protect writers from malicious or self-serving turnabouts in editors' memories (and vice versa), they also help prevent genuine misunderstandings. I once went away from a conference with a newspaper editor thinking he had agreed to pay me $200 per piece for a three-part series on life in China. He combined and condensed two of the three articles I submitted into one longer piece and excerpted the third in a sidebar which ran with it. When I heard that he was paying me $250 for this whole thing, I blew up. But he insisted that he had asked for a "two- or *maybe* three-part series," and when I consulted my memory, I had to admit that that was probably what he had said. So eager was I for the assignment that I apparently mentally revised "two- or *maybe* three-part series" to "three-part series." Nevertheless I insisted that $250 was too little, considering all the work I had put in. We compromised at $300, which he said was more than he could afford. The whole imbroglio might have been prevented by an explicit, detailed agreement in writing.

Another assignment taught me vividly never to be intimidated by a publisher's "standard" contract. After a long get-acquainted conference with an editor, I submitted a query for one of the ideas we had discussed. The managing editor replied, giving me the assignment and enclosing a three-page work-for-hire contract for me to sign. I called the original editor to complain about the contract. "When I asked what rights you generally buy, you didn't say anything about work for hire," I said. I'd rehearsed a spiel on why I wouldn't sign a work-for-hire agreement, but his reply made that unnecessary. "Oh," he said, "she sent you the wrong standard contract; we have several. Hang on, we'll send you another one." I suspect that many other magazines have two or more "standard" sets of contract terms, one for Tina Timmids and another for writers who request better conditions. *Yankee,* commendably, is explicit about this. Each contract form they've sent me contains three options, with escalating fees: the lowest fee for first magazine rights; slightly more for that plus book rights; and slightly more for all rights. If something in a contract offends you, ask for changes; at worst, the editor will stand firm.

A very few publications print their contract terms, such as "work for hire," on the back of their checks, so that the writer is "agreeing" to the terms by endorsing and cashing the check. Some authorities advise that such a "contract" would not hold up in court and that you can evade the terms by writing "for deposit only" and not your signature. Freelancers Franklynn Peterson and Judi Kesselman-Turkel often just cross out the offensive text before they endorse such a check. In any case, it's not only unfair but unforgivably sleazy to inform a writer of policies at payment time, I think; such a publication belongs on writers' blacklists.

WRITING "ON SPEC"

What can you do if you already have moderate to impressive publication credits and a magazine that liked a query of yours asks you to write an article "on spec"? Like many writers, I used to think you'd either have to swallow your pride and risk your time and energy like a beginner or stand on principle and practicality and refuse. But now, edified by the case of the "standard" work-for-hire contract, I see a few other options. One tack would go something like this: "I'm sorry, I don't write on spec anymore. Did you see my credits? I've had assignments from *WW, XX, YY* and *ZZ* magazines. Can I send you more clips? I would really like to do the piece for you, but only on assignment." A less aggressive but perhaps more promising strategy is to send your best clips and ask the editor, "Can you tell me why you're asking me to write on spec? I generally don't. Is it your standard policy for everyone, or are you not sure you like the topic, or are you not sure I can write an acceptable article?" At the very least, the reply should help you figure your odds for that "on spec" article more precisely.

GETTING PAID

Pay on acceptance vs. pay on publication. Try to include a provision for "pay on acceptance" in your contract with a magazine. It means that you will be paid when or a few weeks after the magazine accepts your piece. "Pay on publication," on the other hand, means that you will be paid when or a few weeks after the magazine publishes your piece. Why does this distinction matter? Consider that if a magazine accepts a piece of yours, promising to pay on publication, and then holds it and holds it, your only recourse is to ask for the piece back. By then, it may very well be out of date and your hard work will have been for nothing. On the other hand, if the magazine paid on acceptance and then never publishes the piece, the money you received remains yours.

Kill fee. Most publications that assign articles offer a "kill fee" (also called a "guarantee") of a certain percentage of an article's purchase price (30 to 50 percent, usually) for a professional-quality piece that the publication for some reason decides not to run. No one likes getting kill fees, but they do provide minimal compensation for your time and effort and leave you free to offer your article elsewhere. All rights revert to you when a publication returns your article with a kill fee.

Expenses. Before you zip off to Tahiti to interview a minor source for your assigned article, find out the assigner's expense policy. Most magazines routinely reimburse for long-distance telephone calls and car travel necessary for assigned articles. Larger expenses should be cleared with your editor in advance. Sometimes your contract will specify an expense limit. Smaller expenses, such as paper and postage, are normally considered part of your overhead. Submit an itemized, documented bill for the relevant expenses along with your completed article and you'll usually receive one check for both the purchase price and the expenses for the article. If an assigned article gets "killed," you should receive expenses along with your kill fee.

SAMPLE ASSIGNMENT CONFIRMATION

Stephen Roth signed this letter and sent it back to me promptly. The article appeared as "Editorial Style" in the April 1987 issue of *Personal Publishing*.

SAMPLE ASSIGNMENT CONFIRMATION

December 31, 1986
Stephen Roth, Editor
Personal Publishing
6006 Second Ave., NW
Seattle, WA 98107

Dear Mr. Roth:

Thank you for your call assigning me an article for your magazine. This letter will serve as a confirmation of the terms of the assignment. If I have represented our agreement correctly, please sign one copy of this letter and return it to me. If not, please clarify the misunderstanding.

We have agreed that I will write an article of 1,500–2,500 words, including sidebar(s), on how to develop an editorial style sheet for a publication, due the end of February for your May issue. Pay will be on acceptance at the rate of $50 per printed page (with about 750 words/page).

Good luck in your new location. I look forward to receiving one signed copy of this letter; please keep the other for your files.

Sincerely,

Marcia Yudkin

10 / Mailing and Filing

As a freelancer, you'll do most of your business by mail. Hence it helps to be clear on some postal basics, such as the different classes of mail and particular services like special delivery. Ordinarily you should use first-class mail. If your letter is headed for a distant domestic destination, it will automatically go by air, so you needn't mark it "airmail" or add extra stamps to expedite it. The post office calls first-class packages over a certain weight "priority mail" but processes them at the same speed as first-class letters. Fourth-class mail, reserved for books and manuscripts, costs less but is correspondingly slower and handled less carefully; don't bother with it.

What if you want your message to arrive faster than usual? Deluded by the image of the postman ringing the doorbell, many people think special delivery whooshes letters along. Not really. "Special delivery" means only that *when the mail gets to the final post office,* someone brings it first thing in the morning to the addressee, who must sign for it. The flourish and few hours saved might be worthwhile for a box of chocolates on Valentine's Day, but won't impress a secretary or editor who sees that yours is just another query.

The only class of mail that the U.S. Postal Service delivers faster than first class is Express Mail, with guaranteed next-day delivery. Federal Express and other private companies also offer this service. I use next-day delivery only when I'm up against a deadline and when the magazine to which I'm submitting the piece has agreed to reimburse me.

"Certified mail, return receipt requested," a service I use more often, requires the recipient to sign for the piece and provides proof that it reached its destination. I might want such evidence of delivery for irreplaceable slides or need it for certain letters like one breaking off with an agent or one demanding long-overdue money from a publisher. The absolutely safest way to send anything is registered mail, which the Postal Service keeps locked up at every stage of custody. It's designed for negotiable bonds and other such valuables, but I've used it for a camera-ready manuscript that couldn't easily be redone. If you're ever tempted to insure something you're sending, keep in mind that the Postal Service's idea of "value" for photographs and manuscripts is just the cost of the materials—that is, the film and processing or typing paper.

Although the Postal Service never runs sales or offers discounts on stamps, I can suggest a few ways to save on postage. First, avoid overstamping. I have one friend who sends me manuscripts with as much as one dollar more in stamps than they need. I think she does this because she hates to stand on line at the post office. But if you learn how much postage a ten- or fifteen-page manuscript sealed in a certain kind of envelope requires and keep various denominations of stamps on hand, you won't be tempted to follow her example. (It's also a good idea to find the post office branches with the shortest lines.) Second, try using lighter envelopes. Instead of traditional nine-by-twelve manila clasp envelopes, consider stocking up on the ultralight yet stronger ones made of Tyvek; the weight they save usually more than compensates for their higher cost. Finally, are you using larger envelopes than you need? For up to about eight pages, business-size envelopes, which are much lighter than nine-by-twelves, are fine.

Before I go on to international mailing, I'd like to insert a few words in defense of our oft-maligned U.S. Postal Service. People often talk about important letters "lost in the mail," but in more than seven years of freelancing I have never encountered a verifiable case of an item lost in the mail. Perhaps I'm extraordinarily lucky, but I suspect "lost in the mail," like "I've been trying to call you" (from people who don't know I have an answering machine), is just a handy excuse. On the other hand, my evidence indicates that mail to New York City seems frequently to get bottlenecked and delayed. Allow for this when you calculate probable reply time from a publication in Manhattan.

Since foreign correspondence is considerably more expensive and complicated than domestic, you'll want to take that into account in considering whether or not to approach markets in Britain, Australia, Hongkong, India and so on. Overseas surface mail can take months, so you'd have to pay much higher airmail rates and mark your envelopes "airmail." For foreign submissions, the rule about enclosing an SASE if you want a reply becomes a rule that you must furnish return postage. Must you round up British, Australian, or Hongkong stamps, then, and in what denominations? The international postal community provides a solution in the form of "International Reply Coupons," which your foreign recipients can cash in for stamps usable from their own countries. Though you can buy them at most larger post offices in the United States, most branches that sell the coupons can't tell you how many coupons you should buy for an airmail reply of a given weight from a given country. Because of the expense and uncertainty surrounding International Reply Coupons, I recommend sending disposable copies of manuscripts overseas along with two or three coupons for an airmail yes or no. Don't forget that Canada is a foreign country; Canadian editors will think the worst of you if you put U.S. stamps on an envelope for reply from Canada.

I would never dare send irreplaceable photos abroad, and domestically I never submit photos except when an editor expects them—because some publishers lose track of what arrives in their offices and don't return everything they ought to. When I send slides, I arrange them in plastic display slipcases that cost about twenty cents each at stationery or photo supply stores and tape cardboard protectors around them. The cardboard is important for black-and-white prints as well, and in both cases I write "PHOTOS—DO NOT BEND!" in big letters on both sides of the envelope.

Except for slides that an editor is specifically expecting, never mail your only copy of anything. You'll need a filing and record system for copies of your queries and articles and to keep track of where and when you sent which queries and articles. Instead of depending on photocopy shops, I keep my next-to-last draft of an article with the final corrections on it and a carbon copy of every query letter.

I keep several other kinds of files as well:

• A file with originals of my publications and a running list of them so I can periodically update my résumé.

• A "market" file, with notes, names, addresses and clippings on markets I might want someday to try.

• A file of articles about writing torn out of *Writer's Digest* and *Coda* (the newsletter, recently renamed *Poets & Writers,* of Poets & Writers, Inc.) that I think I can profitably reread from time to time.

• Clippings from newspapers or elsewhere containing ideas and information I might want to follow up on someday for an article.

• A fat file of all my rejection letters, whether nice, infuriating or boring.

• A so-far thin file labeled "fan mail."

• Contracts and notes from phone conversations with editors.

Anybody who's ever seen my worktable can guess that these files are not always completely organized, but I can say that, like the U.S. Postal Service, I very rarely lose something.

11 / Business Details

Many fledgling freelancers don't realize that if they are seriously trying to sell their work, they have the right to consider their writing a business. Thus they miss out not only on certain tax benefits but also on some deductible amenities. At this writing, Congress is still fiddling with some details of the new tax law, so I can only cover some general principles. And since I am not a tax specialist, please check my advice in this chapter against reliable sources of information on current IRS regulations.

Some items and services you purchase for your writing are obviously business expenses: postage, paper and envelopes, typewriter ribbons, copying, *Writer's Market* and, in connection with articles you are writing, long-distance telephone calls, film costs and transportation. Tallying these on the IRS's Schedule C gives you a good deal, because many of the expenses you'd incur whether or not they were deductible. These unavoidable expenses thus help reduce your tax in addition to boosting your career. When you add up your writing income, remember to include any reimbursements for these or other expenses in your gross income.

Some other items you may be more eager to buy when you realize that they're discounted, in effect, by being deductible. A letterhead printed with your name, address and phone number is one example; another is business cards, which you must order in lots of 500. No editor will offer you an assignment simply because of your business stationery or because at an appropriate moment you whipped out a well-designed business card, but these products reinforce your image as a professional. On the other hand, any editor who calls a writer and gets no answer will wonder how serious a freelancer you can be. So if you've hesitated to buy an answering machine, go out and get one now—it's deductible, too. Consider also the stability and convenience of a post office box, which is also deductible. I began using one out of necessity when I had no reliably long-term address, but I discovered distinct advantages to maintaining it afterward as my business address:

• I could move locally without losing any mail. One friend of mine who moved across a town line lost all of her magazine subscriptions for a while.

• When I went away for weeks at a time, the post office automatically saved my mail. Or, by giving friends my key, I could have them check my mail.

• If a piece of mail requiring my signature arrived, I never needed to make a special trip to the post office to pick it up; I was already right there.

• If someone sent something to a long-expired address of mine, the clerks stuck it in my box instead of stamping it "return to sender."

Other legitimate expenses for your writing business that the IRS recognizes: advertising, writing courses and workshops (including, for one that's out of town, transportation, parking, tolls, room and 80 percent of your board), dues for writers' organizations, magazine subscriptions that help your writing, word-processing software, writing books, bank fees if you keep a separate business account, typewriter repairs. If you ever employ a typist or consult a copyright lawyer, their fees would be deductible as well. Starting in 1987, you can deduct 25 percent of health insurance costs for you and your family if you're in business for yourself and neither you nor your spouse are covered by employers. Since 1985 you need to be able to prove that you use your computer and certain other potentially recreational items like cameras and tape recorders for business, not pleasure. Don't forget to list the insurance you pay to protect your business property.

The more expensive, durable equipment that you use in your work, like typewriters, computers and printers, tape recorders, cameras, as well as accoutrements for your work space—bookshelves, desk, lamps, wood stove—fall into a special category and require an additional form, 4562. Because their usefulness extends beyond the current tax year, you are supposed to depreciate these items, that is, spread out their cost according to certain formulas—so much percent deducted for the first year, so much for the second, etc. However, here's where you get a chance to exercise your creativity. Up to a certain limit (as of 1987, $10,000) you can choose to deduct such expenses completely in the current tax year. Doing so is called, appropriately, "expensing." Sometimes you can reduce your business income to zero by expensing. On the other hand, if you depreciate, you generate deductions for future years, when you may have more writing income to offset. The ins and outs of depreciation, as well as many other invaluable tax tips, are explained clearly in the annual *Tax Guide for College Teachers,* which also includes completed sample returns (see Resources for details).

If you work at home or in a rented office, you may be able to deduct utilities and rent or mortgage for that room or section of your house. The qualification is that you must use that area exclusively and regularly for business. However, starting in 1987, you can deduct home office expenses only up to the point that they begin to produce a net loss for your business. Beyond that point you can carry them over to future years. Keep in mind that home office deductions are reportedly more likely than most other items to trigger audits.

As a business, you need to keep legible, systematic records and documentation of your income and expenditures. My record-keeping system consists of an ordinary spiral notebook ruled off in four columns: the date; description of the income or expenditure; a column for amount of money received; a column for amount of money paid. Typical descriptions are just "postage" or "copying" or "from *Yankee.*" If you eat lunch or dinner out for business purposes, add a few more details: "dinner at Epicene with K. Kranz of *Lifestyles* to discuss ballooning article." Similarly, business travel would require dated entries like this: "Norman, Maine: 523 miles round trip to interview Red Rillon for *Field & Stream* article." Get receipts, especially for cash purchases, and file them in a safe place for at least three years. Resist the temptation to throw your rejection letters in the trash; replies from editors will help establish the extent of your business activity if you get audited.

The current rule of thumb for distinguishing a hobby from a business is that a business should clear a profit in three years out of five. (Before tax reform, it was two out of five.) But tax experts cite artists and writers who have successfully claimed a net loss ten years or more in a row. These lucky/unlucky individuals were able to convince the IRS or the tax court that they carried on their business activity in a businesslike manner, with the intention of eventually turning a profit. Still, if your writing generates losses year after year, won't deducting these losses from other income increase your chances of being audited? Keep in mind that, except for some random selection of victims, the IRS usually chooses for audits returns that are likely to justify the time it will take to examine them (and their filers) closely. Unless your writing produces an enormous loss that offsets your spouse's large income, as a beginning writer you are unlikely to fall into that category.

Because I hate to expose my financial choices to strangers, because I can view filling out tax forms as a challenging mathematical/logical puzzle, and because I've found reference guides that explain what I need to know, I've always prepared my own tax returns. If you do decide to use an accountant, ask other self-employed writers or artists in your area to recommend someone familiar with the atypical businesses of freelancers. If you go it alone, don't forget that you may be responsible not only for filing Schedule C and a few others along with your 1040, but also for paying "estimated tax" four times a year.

12 / After Acceptance

When your jubilation at the acceptance of your article begins to wear off, you may think that all that's left will be more or less happy anticipation until your article appears in print. Not so. You should be concerned with one more important step and two possible hitches. Finally, publication day may not be quite what you expect. Forewarned is forearmed.

EDITING

Editors merit their title not because they decide what material to accept and reject but because they edit. At every place but the most slipshod editorial office, you can count on some editor going through your accepted piece to fix vague verbs, ambiguous sentences, unclear transitions and inconsistencies in punctuation. To put your piece into house style, she may adjust the paragraphing and add subheads. At publications that try to avoid page jumps (that is, continuing articles to the end of the magazine with "please turn to page ———"), she may tinker with your article, cutting here and there to fit it into the allotted space. If she believes your piece needs rewriting, she may go ahead and substitute another lead or conclusion, rearrange the parts, modify your diction. Fact-checkers and lawyers may impose other corrections or deletions. Unfortunately, many editors will not notify you in advance about changes they have wreaked.

Being edited has ranged from a pleasant to an agonizing

experience for me. Editors at the *New York Times*, *Ms.* and the *Village Voice* consulted me, by telephone, in a spirit of respectful cooperation about small improvements they wanted to suggest in my prose. In almost every case I agreed that the changes and cuts were reasonable. At the other extreme, an editor at the *Valley Advocate*, without consulting me, rewrote sections of an article on local chiropractors that she had assigned me. When I read the published version I wanted to hide in a closet for a few weeks. It was a first-person article, and she had substituted phrases and words to suggest that I had certain attitudes that I wouldn't have adopted for a million dollars.

Expect that editors will change the title you gave your article, but otherwise you needn't accept that kind of humiliation and anguish as unpreventable bad luck. When you pass in the final manuscript of an article on assignment or on spec, indicate in your cover letter that you would be glad to make changes if they have suggestions for improvement. That's a polite way of implying that they should consult you. If you can think of a reason—say, legally sensitive technicalities—that would make it in the publication's best interest to check changes with you, say so. When I submitted articles about my experiences working in China, I explained that seemingly innocuous changes might trigger trouble for my Chinese colleagues. Also, I asked to proofread my articles to make sure the Chinese names and words were spelled and punctuated properly. Accordingly, *The Progressive* and the *Valley Advocate* (a different editor was now in charge) let me review their final edited computer printout.

If you are lucky enough to see prepublication proofs, resist the temptation to check them comma for comma, word for word against the manuscript as you submitted it. Instead, examine their version carefully for inaccuracies and spots where changes distorted your meaning or spoiled your style. Never call your editor about such problems until you're calm enough to discuss them diplomatically. I've found that usually the editor had some reason to object to my wording, yet was willing to change back or work out a third version if I explained how the editing had introduced a mistake or avoidable awkwardness. You can't always win your point, however. Once I objected to "jelling [of dissatisfaction]" where I had written "gelling," but the former was "house style," so I had to give in. I've encountered magazines and newsletters run by ex-English teachers who refused to print a contraction or a sentence beginning with "But" or "And." Worst of all, and rare at better publications, are editors who think that a good enough reason to rewrite submissions is that they wouldn't have written them exactly that way.

PAYMENT

When your article was assigned, or when it was accepted, the editor should have told you when you could expect payment. Checks don't always arrive according to promises, however. If you've waited several weeks past the due date, it's time to take some action. What can you do to nudge payment in your direction? As your first step, I suggest sending a polite letter to the editor you dealt with about your article and simultaneously something that looks like a bill to the publication's accounting department. Wait two weeks, and if you aren't satisfied with the response, call the editor person-to-person collect and inform him or her, again politely, that you are still waiting. If that doesn't work, then escalate to stronger tactics. Get a lawyer to write the publisher a threatening letter. Or, join the National Writers Union (address in Resources) if you're not already a member and ask its grievance committee for help. With one phone call, they prompted *Ms.* to send me a check which I had been trying to get for four months.

Sometimes, on the other hand, it may not be payment for which you wait and wait but publication. Here there's not much anyone can do for you. Almost always your implicit or explicit contract with a magazine commits it at most to buy and pay for certain rights. A magazine that has bought and paid for first serial rights is not obligated to publish the article. Why would a magazine buy something and then not use it? New developments—technological, political, biographical—could have made the article out of date after you turned it in. One of the magazine's competitors may have "scooped" you, which would make your article look derivative, though it wasn't. The magazine's advertising may have fallen off, forcing the magazine to run fewer articles. Or, although you rewrote your article at the magazine's request and produced a professional-quality piece, the magazine might still not like it, yet it paid anyway, honorbound. Less to their credit, some publications like to overbuy against a sudden dearth of material.

Putting your all into an article that is accepted and then never published is always disappointing. My piece called "China's Nap Reform," which I "sold" to the op-ed page of the *Boston Globe*, never ran. No glory, no pay, and because it was tied to current events, I lost the chance to sell it elsewhere. Another time *Yankee* paid me for an assigned profile of a local artist, who happened also to be my friend, and then didn't run it the month or the season it was written for. My friend had been anticipating a blaze of publicity for her work and took the blow hard.

Usually, though, what has been accepted will appear in print. Most magazines send contributors at least one free copy of the issue in which their article appears. Newspapers usually send "tearsheets"—actual pages torn from the whole paper. If you've sold a piece to a high-circulation magazine or a newspaper, you may spot your article at a newsstand before your contributor's copies or tearsheets arrive in your mailbox. You'll stare at the by-line, drink in your words and finally stumble around town expecting acquaintances to congratulate you and strangers to ask for your autograph.

Here too you'd be better off not having such hopeful expectations. Generally when an article of mine appears in a large-circulation national magazine like *Ms.* I hear nothing right away, even from friends who subscribe. It seems some people let magazines pile up for months on their coffee tables, and others, believe it or not, pay no attention whatsoever to by-lines. Bookstore clerks don't blink when they look at my checks, nor do former colleagues who read the article and like it let me know until they happen to run into me—sometimes months later. Try not to draw negative conclusions if no one calls you or stops you on the street and your mailbox does not fill up with fan letters. On the other hand, I twice met people who remembered an article of mine and told me of the impact it had had on them—four years later. I prefer that kind of impact to being a five-minute, phone-ringing-off-the-hook celebrity.

13 / Productive Work Habits

During the second half of the year I worked in China, the Foreign Languages Press, my employer, assigned me the task of writing a short book on private business in China's cities. Although I wondered if I could really finish the interviewing, analysis, synthesis and writing of the book before I was scheduled to go home, I accepted the opportunity enthusiastically. Around the beginning of May, having gathered almost all the information I needed, I drafted a chapter outline and went downstairs to discuss it with Zhao Yihe, my boss.

"Oh, by the way," he added after he had approved the outline and advised me to write it from the American point of view. "We have a lot of things we have to get ready for the thirty-fifth anniversary of the country, in October. When do you think you can finish the first draft?" By now I felt pretty confident I could finish before I went home. "I can guarantee the whole thing will be finished by the beginning of September." He literally almost fell off his chair.

"I mean the whole thing, not just the first draft," I hastened to add. He reseated himself and, looking away, took a swig of tea. "But the first draft—when can you finish that? How many pages will it be?" "About 150," I guessed. "So, how many pages can you write in one day? Ten?" *Ten?* Now I was shocked. "No . . ." "Five?" "Less. Look, you shouldn't rush me. I want to do a good job." "Okay, but I think you can get it done faster than you think," he said. I left his office feeling sick. Though

Zhao had an American master's degree in journalism and was a skilled, astute editorial director, he seemed to think a book could be spewed out as forcefully and steadily as water in a motorized fountain. I had gone in proud that I was going to accomplish something I wasn't sure was possible. It took me a while to recover from Zhao's implication that the fastest I could write was very, very slow.

What this story says to me now is that trying to live up to anyone else's idea of productivity can be destructive. No matter how pleased you are with your progress, if you're not alert to this danger, someone may come along and puncture your balloon. If you can write ten pages a day, a scoffer can deflate you with *"Only* ten? Harrison Bowles writes twenty a day." When the newspaper publicizes the fellow who wrote a 300-page novel in ten days, Harrison Bowles in turn might get a sinking feeling of inadequacy. And even that ten-day wonder might be vulnerable to despair at the news of the genius who in ten days wrote a 300-page novel that is an undisputed masterpiece.

I suggest, then, that you set your own realistic daily, monthly or annual goals and define productivity in terms of progress and a schedule of completion that corresponds to your own work style, experience and available time. After all, except when you or your children depend totally on your writing income (more on that in Chapter 15), as a freelancer you *can* aim for the pace that suits you. But why set any goals at all? I believe they help, both mentally and materially. When I embarked on my dissertation, my first long writing project, I calculated that if I could produce one good page each weekday, I could finish the whole project in well under a year. After several months of writing, I easily upped daily production to two pages. As part of my bargain with myself, as soon as I had finished my daily quota, I could leave the library and swim, play music, read novels or do whatever I felt like doing with a clear conscience. A decade later, I still pretty much hold to a two-or-three-pages-a-day-then-play standard, whether I'm writing a book or short pieces. And I now have some grasp of why that regime works.

The secret of productive writing—that is, meeting your own realistic goals—lies, I believe, in making efficient use of both discipline and inspiration. Relying on inspiration only, you probably won't finish half of what you could if you added a dose of discipline. Grinding along on sheer discipline, on the other hand, you probably aren't getting the sparks of life, fun or wisdom into your work that you could if you knew how to mobilize your resources of inspiration. By discipline I mean more consistency and clarity of purpose than grim nose-to-the-grindstone work, and by inspiration I don't necessarily mean mystical visitations of the muse. Though the two factors are intertwined in a productive working style, I'll discuss them separately, discipline first.

Establishing the habit of writing regularly, regardless of your mood or other responsibilities or temptations, is probably the best favor you can do yourself if you're serious about writing. The habit will bear the most fruit if you can schedule it for your peak thinking period, that time of day when your mind is most energetic and nimble. I usually start my workday before 9 A.M. and go for four or five hours. For me, insights, metaphors, connections come more effortlessly then than in late afternoon; after dinner until bedtime I can rarely concentrate on serious reading, much less put ideas together logically. But some other people I know can hardly write a sentence before 9 P.M. and think best from then until halfway to dawn. While I haven't seen scientific evidence of this, I suspect that these predilections are as genetic and unchangeable as right-handedness and left-handedness. In any case, find your peak time and use it well.

Using your peak time well involves eliminating interruptions and distractions as far as possible during that period of time. Take a lesson from the misfortune of Samuel Coleridge, whose long, brilliant poem "Kubla Khan" came to him whole during a dream; a visitor rang while Coleridge was in the midst of transcribing it, and by the time he was done dealing with the visitor, he (and we) had lost the rest of the poem forever. Train your friends, roommates and family not to bother you during your writing hours. Turn on your answering machine or respond to all calls with a mere "Can I call you back later?" Don't make appointments with doctors, car mechanics, cabinetmakers, barbers or hairdressers during those hours if you can help it.

But what if your working conditions aren't ideal? Maybe you don't have any space at home for a desk. Or maybe the sirens, screaming neighbors or your own children rarely quiet down enough for you to work. Or perhaps your children or your business need constant attention and you can't afford regular help. These problems really can derail your writing. My own nightmare situation is music-loving neighbors. If I hear a beat, however hushed, it swats rhythmically at my thoughts, wrecking any chance for concentration. If any of these difficulties afflict you, you'll have to put high priority on finding a creative solution. (Consider borrowing an office, bartering, building a cork-lined room . . .)

Taking a disciplined approach to your writing doesn't mean forcing yourself to sit and stare at your computer screen or writing paper for a certain number of hours nonstop, no matter what. Here's where methods to cultivate inspiration come in. When you feel yourself slowing down, or when you feel stuck, get up and do something mindless for ten or fifteen minutes. Putter around the kitchen, spy on your neighbors, feed the fish, eat some chocolates. Though this may look like you're wasting time, actually you're not. During the break your subconscious mind continues working on the problem your conscious mind was struggling with before you got up. Indeed, studies show that many renowned scientists and artists owe their greatest discoveries to insights that burst on them after they had given up attacking their problem head-on.

In order for the break to bear fruit, however, you may need to convince the people around you that despite the appearance of piddling you *are* still working; the rule against substantive interruptions should still hold. My very worst living situation reached its crisis point over this issue. Reluctantly my housemate agreed not to play her stereo between certain hours, Monday through Friday. Once, during the designated hours, I got stuck and decided to put the problem on hold by taking a shower. My housemate took this as a sign that I had knocked off early and blasted her favorite album at ear-splitting volume. The ensuing quarrel convinced me I should live on peanut butter if that's what it took to afford my own apartment.

Not only during short breaks, but also from one day to the next, when you're working regularly on a single project, your subconscious often continues clicking away on your enterprise while you're otherwise engaged. I think that's why it's usually easier at the beginning of a writing session to see a way to go on than it was at the end of the previous day. Thus, given fifteen hours a week to devote to their writing, most people would accomplish more by spreading the time over five or seven days than using it all up in two.

Taking their cue from Ernest Hemingway, some writing instructors predict that you'll find it easier to start writing the next day if you stopped the day before in the middle of a sentence. The theory is that instead of having to agonize over what should come next, you can just complete the unfinished sentence and go right on. Perhaps your mind works like Hemingway's; mine doesn't. I make the most progress when I stop and start by section. That is, I may be able to pick right up from an uncompleted sentence, but if it leads three or four sentences later to the end of a chapter, or to a point where I need to introduce a new topic, I'm likely to flounder. Stopping at the end of a section helps my subconscious "incubate" the next creative chunk.

Meditation is another method you might want to try to increase your flow of ideas. One business writer I know visualizes a potential reader in vivid detail to help him write for a particular audience. Others have a mental "teacher" they regularly consult for advice. While I can't prescribe any specific program that will work for everyone, it might be worth your while to investigate intuitive techniques and trainings that will help you court inspiration successfully and on a regular basis.

14 / Building Momentum

When you break into print, it will most likely be because of what you have to say, not who you are or (by definition) your previous publications. But eventually you'll probably notice that certain opportunities don't necessarily go to the best queriers but to people who are known and/or proven. Not long ago *Esquire* sent novelist Jay McInerny, not any old Rolling Stones fan, to interview Mick Jagger. The *New York Times* "Sophisticated Traveler" section invites the most well known writers, not just anyone who's lived or gone abroad, to recount their love of Venice or encounters with Sherpas in Hongkong. On a more mundane level, assignments with kill fees go to writers who can back up impressive queries with proof that they've delivered well in the past. As a friend of mine puts it, "Them that gots, gets."

But why react to this truth with envy or resentment? Think of it this way: success breeds success. It's a principle you can put to work at any level of the writing profession. Some applications, such as enclosing or mentioning clips with your queries, are pretty obvious. Less obvious strategies to develop skill and promise into a career include capitalizing on apparent failures. Many of my most surprising breaks may look like luck but actually were the result of a conscious plan to build on what I've already accomplished.

After my first article appeared in the *New York Times,* for example, I migrated to the San Francisco Bay area and tried to scheme up other coups. Since I had academic credentials and experience in reading and analyzing books, book reviews seemed worth a try. I wrote to the *San Francisco Review of Books:* Would they be interested in a review of Susan Griffin's just-published *Pornography and Silence?* I explained my background in the letter, and the editor immediately wrote back "yes" with a deadline and optimal word count. There was no pay, but four months later I had a published book review.

Since the subject area I had tackled was feminist theory, I sent *Ms.* a clipping, asking them to keep me in mind for similar reviews. Some time later, a *Ms.* editor called me. "Your review of Susan Griffin has been floating around our office, and we think it's brilliant," she said. "We commissioned two reviews that weren't satisfactory, and we'd like to reprint yours." Not only did *Ms.* pay me $150 for something I'd originally done for nothing, Griffin's publisher quoted my review prominently in an ad in the *New York Review of Books* and on the back cover of the paperback edition. Free, prestigious publicity!

The general advice I would extract from this experience is to consider using local or nonpaying outlets as a tryout. If your ambition is a national syndicated column, see if you can interest the editor of your community newspaper or perhaps of an organizational newsletter to give you space for a few issues. Since any syndicate will want proof that you can deliver consistently as well as generate good material, a series of clips may help your case more than one isolated triumph. In addition you may learn from the practice and get some helpful feedback. If you do try this strategy, don't forget the possibility of offering your tryout clips or rewritten versions to larger markets for reprint.

Another bizarre incident involved my short story "Bonds," based on the making of the Quabbin Reservoir in central Massachusetts. When I wrote the story I had *Yankee* in mind as a market. *Yankee* held it for two months and then rejected it with a nice personal letter that suggested I try literary magazines. Three years and sixteen more rejections later, I was firming up a different (nonfiction) assignment for *Yankee* when the editor added, "Oh, and by the way, that Quabbin story you sent us a few years ago—?" "Ye-es—?" I prompted, sure that she would say not to make this article like that story. After all, they'd rejected it. "John Pierce, our managing editor, wants to take another look at it." "You mean he remembers it?" I was in shock. "You mean *Yankee* might buy it now?" "No promises," the editor cautioned. Two weeks later, though, *Yankee* sent me a contract for the story.

It turned out that originally "Bonds" had aroused strong enthusiasm and strong dislike. Later, with a change of personnel, partisans of the story were able to vote it through. The lesson was not only that a rejected story can linger in the minds of editors but, again, that it pays to follow through on each personal response you get from editors until your submissions or queries establish a real two-way relationship. I doubt that *Yankee* would have bought "Bonds" had I not kept trying to sell them other work, and the way I broke into the *Village Voice* reinforces this. Thulani Davis, an editor there, liked a query of mine although she rejected it. I sent another, about war tax resistance, but couldn't get an answer from her. The story came out instead in the *Valley Advocate* and *In These Times.* I sent Thulani Davis a clip and got the following phone call not long afterward: "I liked your piece a lot and I'm sorry we couldn't publish it. We're putting together a special issue on nuclear disarmament and I wonder if you have any ideas for it." Did I! (I was a peace activist.) A short article I wrote about the Children's Campaign for Nuclear Disarmament appeared in the *Voice*'s special issue for the historic June 12, 1982 disarmament rally.

I've also twice transformed downright failure into honors and opportunities. Although the magazine that commissioned a piece on the New England School for Nannies rejected it, I was pretty sure it was well written. I entered it in the 1986 *Writer's Digest* writing competition: I won honorable mention. Simultaneously I sent it to the editor of *Travel and Learning Abroad,* who asked writers wishing to be considered for assignments to submit pre-edited copy. Months later he contacted me and specifically mentioned the nannies article as having impressed him.

Try to recycle your failures, then; you may learn that what bores one editor fascinates another. And note the opportunity presented by contests. I don't usually submit rejected material but rather take contests as a challenge to develop ideas lingering in the back of my mind. In graduate school I worked something up for a college prize for the best essay on women and not only won $100 but got the article published in a feminist journal. Just before I turned thirty I wrote up my thoughts on the arms race for *The Humanist*'s essay contest for under-thirties and won $500 and publication. I have my eye now on several fiction contests with a 2,000-word limit. Normally I write longer, but I can stretch my skills by trying rich compression.

Another principle for building momentum is branching out. Originally I tried writing nonfiction as a diversion from fiction, but to my surprise, nonfiction brought more immediate rewards, including more challenge, satisfaction and renown than I had anticipated. Publishing led to teaching writing, which in turn led to the work you now hold in your hands. Earlier, once I had honed my ability to write, I developed editing as another sideline. The editing experience helped me land my one-year job writing and editing in China, which provided material for more than fifteen articles and a book.

When you do get something accepted, provide the editor with a brief "bio note" designed to spark interest in your work in progress. Editors and agents do write or call people whose work impresses them if it seems they might have a book, a mini-series or a movie in them. But if you're sticking to articles for the moment, don't worry about snagging an agent; the 10 to 15 percent of your article fees, which is all reputable agents charge, won't be worth their while. On the other hand, if you do hope to write a book, you can test the waters and build credibility for publishers with an article or, even better, a series of them.

Finally, you should never stop trying to learn and increase your skills. Study and analyze unusually well written or memorable articles. Try writers' conferences, workshops, classes and groups. I've found the big conferences both instructive and destructive, and local workshops more useful in hooking me up with like-minded writers interested in exchanging work. If you're lucky you'll find an ideal critic who understands what you are trying to do and pinpoints the spots in your work where you haven't—yet—accomplished it.

Learning to improve as a writer includes learning about yourself as well. Take stock: what are your strengths and weaknesses as a freelancer? Instead of dwelling on your mistakes and failures, think of what they can teach you. As the Buddhists put it, "make the hindrances part of your path." And don't let yourself get stuck repeating small accomplishments once you've learned how to make them come easily. Keep reaching for challenges that will propel you one stage further toward goals that were once sheer daydreams.

15 / Finding Your Own Path

"Success at any price" is not my motto. In particular I don't urge what Virginia Woolf called "adultery of the brain." Prostituting one's talents to the highest, most prestigious or only bidder is not ultimately satisfying. But I don't have many rules to offer for avoiding that. If we define writing with integrity as remaining true to one's own values, what counts in this respect will differ from person to person. More generally, only you can decide what place freelance writing ought to have in your life, whether it will become your primary endeavor or a supplement to other things you do. Aim to find your own path to success, as *you* define success, and keep in mind that you'll probably feel your way through by trial and error.

Once, halfway through a writer's conference where participants spent mornings in small groups headed by well-known writers, a woman begged the group I was in to let her switch into it. "I can't go back to my group," she said. "I write light, that's what I do and want to do—Erma Bombeck–type pieces that people can identify with, that make people smile. What's wrong with that? But [the leader] was completely unsympathetic, even nasty, about it." We welcomed the woman and gave her feedback on her humor pieces that accepted the premises of the genre. I shudder to think of the deformation of talent that might have resulted if she had agreed with that arrogant writer's invalidation of her aim.

Where that woman knew that light writing was her forte, I had to learn that I couldn't mask my relatively serious attitude toward life. I pitched a piece on the New England School for Nannies to a certain regional magazine although a good half of its articles appeal to a sophisticated in-group contemptuous of tacky outsiders. (I would write for its better side, I thought.) Perhaps I should have balked at the editor's instruction to "give the piece a light, ironic touch" but I took that as a challenge. After my research, however, I couldn't figure out how to be ironic without making fun of the nannies-in-training, which I didn't want to do. I made the piece as light as clean puffs of cotton, and here was the verdict: "well reported but earnest and without the spark of fun or wit that we're looking for." My verdict: if *that* was earnest, then I'd better forget about trying to break into that magazine. Making the piece that light had already demanded contortions; making it frivolous enough would have required forcing myself to the point of damage.

But I still hadn't learned how to really scrutinize the sensibility of a magazine before querying it. Several months after the nanny article fiasco, I offered a martial-arts magazine an article on how acupuncture had changed in its journey to the West. This was information that I had and wanted to communicate, and according to my scrutiny of the writers' guidelines and a sample issue, my angle seemed appropriate for that magazine. Its editor indeed gave me the assignment and I provided the article and photos. When I received my contributor's copies, however, I was appalled at the violent images and ads for brutal weapons that surrounded my article. Either the sample issue I'd seen was atypical or, more likely, I hadn't looked closely enough at it, relying on my acquaintance with Tai Chi Chuan and Aikido, which focus on harmony and empowerment. So ashamed was I at the setting of the article that I couldn't bear to send copies to the professionals I'd quoted, as I'd promised.

Eventually I realized that for all the importance of market savvy and professionalism, if I didn't give due weight to my personal values my writing "success" would feel hollow, or worse. My freelance writing students helped reinforce this with persistent questions about whether or not they should write for magazines that they didn't like. I came up with three considerations that should help settle doubts about whether or not to try a particular publication:

1. Do you want to communicate certain information or ideas to that particular audience?

2. Do you feel you can communicate with that audience without pretending you are someone you're not?

3. Would you feel comfortable about your friends, relatives and colleagues seeing your work in that publication?

If your answer to any of these questions is "no," then you probably shouldn't query or submit to that market. You may very well find, on the other hand, specific reasons for writing for a magazine that you would never subscribe to or ordinarily read.

Professionals, academics and other highly educated types often feel conflict when they contemplate writing for general audiences. Though they want to disseminate advice, opinions or knowledge beyond their peers, they worry that they will have to "write down"—impart a superficial version of their ideas in tasteless language. I believe that producing a lively, readable, comprehensible article is rarely a matter of compromising yourself. On the contrary, the process will probably teach you how to improve your professional writing as well. Remember that the aim is communication and that most of the principles for engaging and sustaining a reader's interest—a likable voice, examples and lucid sentence structure—apply to any sort of writing. Still, if you do find yourself "writing down," watch out. It can become a perilous habit. I once talked with a former social scientist who had been working for a daily newspaper for four years. "No one cares about the quality of what you do," she complained. "The worse the better sometimes." I got the impression that she had lost the will to craft something up to her own standards and felt doomed in her job, demoralized.

To avoid desecrating your principles, I suggest that whenever you feel the stirrings of conscience, however faint, pause and listen. There may be certain stories you ought to leave alone. One freelancer I know turned down the chance to cover for a national women's magazine a child custody battle where the father had been accused of child abuse, because of her unsubstantiated hunch that neither parent's statements were completely true. Another wanted to write about two men he admired, Guatemalan refugees given sanctuary by a local church, but he had to confront the possibility that lauding them in print would prompt the Immigration and Naturalization Service to deport the men to the murderous situation they had fled. Should you slam with a scathing review a book you thought was awful? Some writers, like John Irving, won't. My version of this is that I hate describing people I've interviewed in unflattering terms. Once I profiled a very sweet scientist who must have weighed almost 300 pounds. My editor rejected my characterization of him as "enormous"—too vague; I agonized over a substitute. Also, I don't like using interviewing tricks like pretending you already know something so the subject will confirm your guess, though such ruses do work.

Should that ex-social scientist have quit her newspaper job, then? "It's a secure job," she said. "I'd like to get out, but . . ." I couldn't tell her—or you—that freelancing is very secure. It's not. Indeed, if you are considering quitting your job and freelancing full-time, I would advise you not to unless you have the equivalent of six to nine months' income saved up. You have to generate a certain volume of queries to drum up business, and it takes time for either writing on assignment or direct submissions to bring the checks into your mailbox. Even so, the checks rarely can be orchestrated to come regularly. When I was beginning to freelance full-time, I sold a story and got paid for two short articles within the space of a month. I multiplied the $1,200 I received that month by twelve and thought, "Hey, I'm out of poverty!" The next two months, of course, much less arrived in my mailbox. That's the nature of the business. Most full-time writers, even those as famous as Joseph Heller, report some lean times.

You may find, like me, that a combination of part-time freelancing with a part-time job (for me, teaching) or sidelines (for me, editing) suits you better than full-time freelancing. Or, with certain skills—say, carpentry or computer programming— you may be able to alternate years or half-years of writing and nonwriting. For most writers I've known, the pressure to keep bringing in enough to buy food and pay the rent or mortgage is not productive. John Gardner once wrote, "The best way a writer can find to keep himself going is to live off his (or her) spouse." Obviously, that won't work for everyone. But I think he's right that before you try to live off your writing you ought to have developed some sort of realistic plan.

There are other decisions you'll have to make. Will you specialize or write on whatever strikes your fancy? Will you aim for a local audience or shoot for the big national magazines as soon as possible? Will you try to exploit everything you do for your writing or keep certain areas of your life to yourself? (I've found I prefer to travel without thinking about anything besides enjoying myself and relaxing.) I encourage you not to follow someone else's formula but to create your own.

16 / Succeeding as a Writer

I have a short and a long answer to the question of what it takes to break into print and keep on getting published. Briefly, it takes humility, confidence and persistence. Humility, so that you can accept criticism and improve your writing to a professional level and beyond; confidence, so you don't crumple at rejection letters as proof of stupidity or ineptitude; and persistence, so you keep on sending out queries and submissions that eventually result in publications. All three qualities characterize the successful freelancer. With humility and confidence only, the would-be writer may give up, rationalizing that she *would* have succeeded if she'd kept on. With confidence and persistence but no humility, the neophyte barrels on, making the same mistakes time after time. And with humility and persistence only, the novice can easily fall into an ineffective take-pity-on-poor-unpublished-me attitude.

But my short answer may make it seem as if these are inborn qualifications that some people have and others lack. Not so. People do change. I can take criticism and learn from my mistakes now, but until my late twenties I had no humility whatsoever. And I have seen fearful, easily discouraged friends slowly gain confidence and persistence. On the other hand, I've heard and read about cocksure writers who hustled themselves to the top of the best-seller lists and then completely lost their nerve. Also, I don't mean to imply that with those three qualities, success is inevitable. A great many other qualities, not all of which we can name, are necessary for a stellar writing career.

So my short answer only begins to approach the truth.

Instead of cataloging qualities, my long answer claims that freelance writing, like Chinese calligraphy, conscientious teaching or maintaining a motorcycle, involves one's whole being. When someone with writing skill and market savvy fails, we can often find a reason in a pattern that holds throughout his or her personality. Obstacles range much more widely than the proverbial "writer's block." Tony is afraid to admit it when he doesn't understand something, so his interviews yield incoherent, garbled explanations that horrify editors and fact-checkers. Peggy arrives late for movies, appointments and with assignments, and turns scathingly bitter when boyfriends, doctors and editors, irritated with her excuses, drop her. Mark, who assumes everyone means him well, never asks about or negotiates pay or kill fees and often ends up getting little or no money for his work. My own nemesis is hating to put the finishing touches on many things I do, including my writing.

The roots of these problems can run very deep. In my own case, after I began selling articles and stories, I noticed that I often sent things off too soon, before they had gone through a sufficient number of revisions. My comment to myself was "I'm too impatient." I tried to restrain my impatience, to force myself to wait and keep rewriting. But I began to notice that in other areas besides my writing I habitually neglected the finishing touches. When I did the dishes, I would inevitably leave the last pot to soak; when I scrubbed the stove top, I would let "almost clean" be clean enough. But when I took on the task of compiling a new edition of the *Guidebook for Publishing Philosophy* for the American Philosophical Association, I decided to conquer this tendency once and for all. As an exercise, I would do this one thing as well as I possibly could—no excuses allowed. All went smoothly until the very end, when my APA contact listed a series of mistakes that remained in my camera-ready manuscript. My resolve weakened; I wanted to correct all of the errors except one. Indeed, when I thought about fixing everything, I felt a resistance so strong as to be almost panic. I was terrified, I realized, to create something perfect.

Why should I have such a strong fear of perfection? I sat down, closed my eyes and asked myself when this fear started. All the images that arose involved the classroom where I went to sixth grade, more than twenty years earlier. I heard voices telling me things like, "You can't draw a perfect circle because then you'd be perfect and no one's perfect." I must have absorbed the belief that if I did something perfect, I'd be inhuman—dead! No wonder perfection frightened me. Recently at a college where I was teaching expository writing I recognized another element in this pattern. Twice my worst student, dropping by to pick up my comments on her paper draft, waved off my carefully phrased assessments with, "Oh yeah, I didn't put very much time into it." Her nonchalance startled me into realizing that my avoidance of perfection was a similar self-protective ploy. If I really put my all into something, I would be defenseless against criticism.

While I'm not a trained psychologist, I can sketch some techniques for pinpointing and overcoming psychological pitfalls that I've observed to work. The best way to begin is to team up with another writer whom you trust and whose difficulties and accomplishments differ from yours. Although you can also try this method alone, the two of you will more easily see through each other's excuses and help by refusing to see the other's plight as inevitable.

First, identify the problem—procrastination, reluctance to go national after becoming a local star, inability to phone editors or sources, whatever. Next, look for a pattern; prompt your memory for other times when you confronted the same or a similar obstacle. Then, as specifically as possible, try to name the particular fears and beliefs that hulk in your way like implacable monsters. You may find surprising results from this step. For example, after my book *Making Good: Private Business in Socialist China* was published in China, I decided that I ought to try to get it reviewed and publicize it in this country.

But even after I'd obtained extra copies of the book, I just didn't want to write up a press release and send copies out with the books. Was I afraid of publicity? Not really, because when strangers praised and promoted my work I felt happy. What I hated and feared was, precisely, promoting my own work myself.

Sometimes just putting a name to your demon cuts it down to manageable size. Other times, the label makes the whole pattern clearer. Once I called my problem "fear of promoting myself," I could connect it with another incident years before. Almost as soon as I finished talking with the *New York Times* education editor who accepted my first article, a man from another department of the paper called about arranging a photo session. "But wait a minute," I replied. "I'm not sure I want to have my picture in the *New York Times.*" He gave an incredulous laugh and asked what could be wrong with having my picture in the *New York Times*. "Well, it's too publicity-seeking," I explained. He retorted, "No more than writing the article in the first place," and worked out a compromise with me: I would be photographed not alone, but with my students. Putting this fear of publicity together with the later incident, I had to admit that my attitude was peculiar and irrational. What *was* wrong, to me, with seeking publicity for oneself? My next step was to search for the root of the attitude. Often you'll discover that the first instance of the pattern that you can recall holds the key to your impediment. When had I seen publicity seeking bring on disaster?

At this point, I could easily finger the source of the problem. Throughout my childhood, I wrote cute, rhymed poems that my parents, relatives and teachers praised profusely. Somehow I or my mother arranged for me to read my verse on a local TV show for kids—twice. Confirmation of my talent, right? I didn't see it that way in seventh grade when I transferred to a more elite school system where the brightest students wrote ultrasophisticated free verse full of dark images that were utterly beyond me. Listening to their creations, I felt exposed, betrayed and ashamed. In retrospect I believed I'd made a fool of myself by ignorantly presenting myself as "talented." I'd long been aware that these events explained my adult avoidance of poetry. But now I saw other ramifications. Clearly, my later avoidance of publicity seeking was designed to prevent a repeat of my seventh-grade humiliation. And just as clearly, this covert motive held the power to sabotage my writing career.

But how to defuse a persistent fear after you uncover the source of its power? First, you can take a deep breath and plunge right through the fear. Each time you summon the courage to bark "Yeah, so what?" to your dread, you erode its strength. I used this tactic when I had that stack of China books on my desk. Next time, I'll go through much less agony to repeat that step and face the challenge beyond: following up. Second, you can try to retrain your subconscious. Lawrence Block, in *Write for Your Life*, suggests counteracting negative beliefs with repeated oral and written affirmations—for my case, something like, "Publicity always brings deserved praise for my work." Henriette Anne Klauser, in *Writing on Both Sides of the Brain*, proposes that you can bring on success more easily by imagining, in great detail, a scenario where you effortlessly go through those difficult steps and receive praise and rewards. Third, with some cleverness and help from friends, you can sometimes scheme a way to bypass your obstacle. When a friend of mine admitted that she could never bring herself to send her finished articles out, we struck a deal: I would go to her house, put each piece in an envelope and address, stamp and mail it for her. Another friend needed deadlines to finish his book; I supplied them and kept after him as if he'd signed a contract with me.

Since everyone has a unique personal history, each person will have different bogeys to identify and disarm in order to keep making progress as a freelance writer. Like life itself, freelancing is a never-ending adventure, challenging, requiring and promoting your development as a human being. The more you recognize this, the greater your chances of reaping rewards from your writing and feeling good about it. As I've argued throughout this book, communicating in print responsibly and successfully demands a lot from you. But if you pursue your goal with wits, character and professionalism, you can very likely inspire, inform, amuse or enlighten the people you want to reach. The prospects are unlimited. Once you find your stride, I predict, freelance writing will continue to bring you joy (not without attendant agony), self-knowledge and fulfillment.

An Annotated List of Resources for Freelance Writing

Market Guides

Allen, Martha Leslie, ed., *Index/Directory of Women's Media.* 3306 Ross Place, NW, Washington, DC 20008: Women's Institute for Freedom of the Press. Annual.

Lists 525 periodicals for women, sorted by zip code and country, amidst a wealth of other resource material on women and the media.

Burack, Sylvia K., ed., *The Writer's Handbook.* Boston: The Writer, Inc. Annual.

One hundred chapters of writing advice, ranging from superficial pep talks to very useful ideas and experiences, and around 200 pages of market listings. Each listing is sparser than those in *Writer's Market,* but some magazines and publishers missed by the latter are included here.

Directory of Publishing Opportunities in Journals & Periodicals, 5th ed. Chicago: Marquis Academic Media, 1981.

Contains information on nearly 4,000 magazines and journals, mainly North American, in all fields. Designed with authors in mind, includes short description, manuscript requirements, reporting time and payment. Good subject index. Can help you find a home for semi-scholarly articles.

Fulton, Len, ed., *The International Directory of Little Magazines and Small Presses.* Paradise, CA: Dustbooks. Annual.

Addresses, phone numbers, subscription prices, editorial needs and payment of over 4,000 little magazines and small presses. Regional index and better subject index than any other market guide. Some sample headings: Adirondacks; anarchist; Armenian; Bilingual; Joseph Conrad; cooking.

Gage, Diane, and Marcia Hibsch Coppess, *Get Published: Editors from the Nation's Top Magazines Tell You What They Want.* New York: Henry Holt, 1986.

Less current than *Writer's Market* and covers only eighty-nine larger consumer, organizational and in-flight magazines, but includes the following information not routinely included in *Writer's Market:* kill fees; classification of types of articles with word length and pay range for each; profile of the typical reader; number of accepted articles out of the number of queries and submissions; rundown on columns open to freelancers; chatty tips from editors.

Gale Directory of Publications. Detroit: Gale Research Co. Annual. Formerly *Ayer Directory of Publications.*

Lists U.S. and Canadian newspapers and magazines geographically; subject indexes. Set up primarily for potential advertisers; gives circulation and frequency, but no other information about publications for contributors. Separate section provides names (and phone numbers) of feature editors of major newspapers.

International Writers' and Artists' Yearbook. Cincinnati, OH: Writer's Digest Books. Annual.

The British counterpart of *Writer's Market.* Lists English-language book, play, broadcast and magazine markets in Great Britain, Australia, Canada, India, Ireland, New Zealand and some African countries, along with advice and information on copyright, taxes, etc., applicable mainly to Britons.

Katz, Bill, and Linda Sternberg Katz, *Magazines for Libraries,* 5th ed. New York: Bowker, 1986.

Describes for librarians some 6,500 periodicals, from popular to scholarly, under 136 subject headings. Lists address, scope, audience, purpose and other information for each; sometimes compares competing magazines.

Literary Market Place. New York: Bowker. Annual.

Lists information on book publishers, literary agents, writers' associations, writers' conferences, literary grants and prizes and editorial services. Every library I've ever visited has a copy, often kept behind the librarian's desk.

Magazine Industry Market Place. New York: Bowker. Annual.

Lists more than 3,000 magazines, including addresses, phone numbers, personnel, frequency of publication, date founded and circulation.

Also lists new magazines and others that recently ceased publication. Subject index, but no submission information.

O'Gara, Elaine, *Travel Writer's Markets*. P.O. Box 7548, Berkeley, CA 94707: Winterbourne Press, 1987. Periodically updated.

Most reliable, comprehensive resource for marketing travel articles. Includes tax tips and details on more than 400 magazines and newspapers that buy travel pieces, and just as important, lists those that are not presently buying anything from freelancers and those that have recently quit publishing altogether.

Writer's Market. Cincinnati, OH: Writer's Digest Books. Annual, comes out every September.

Indispensable yearly investment. A guide to (mainly) trade book publishers, general and specialized magazines and some Sunday newspaper magazine sections. Includes editors' names, submission details, range of pay and how to prepare manuscripts and queries, keep records for taxes and protect your rights in your work.

Periodicals

Byline. P.O. Box 130596, Edmond, OK 73013. Monthly.

A worthwhile service magazine for serious beginning writers. How-to articles, markets, experiences, contests.

Folio: The Magazine for Magazine Management. Box 4949, Stamford, CT 06907.

The *Publishers Weekly* for magazine publishers. Check it, if your library has it, for news about magazine startups.

Publishers Weekly. R. R. Bowker Co., 205 E. 42nd St., New York, NY 10017. Weekly.

Nearly everyone in the book publishing world, and most libraries, subscribe to this for news of books, publishing trends and noteworthy writers, agents, editors and publishers.

Travelwriter Marketletter. Room 1723, The Plaza Hotel, New York, NY 10019. Monthly.

Expensive but worth every dollar, even if you're not primarily a travel writer. Tells who's buying what, who's changed what policy, who's not paying, and who is starting or considering starting a new magazine.

Utne Reader. 2732 West 43rd St., Minneapolis, MN 55410. Bimonthly.

The *Reader's Digest* of alternative/progressive/small magazines. Aside from its provocative articles, contains two features of particular interest to freelancers: "Some of a Kind," reviews of publications in one subject area, and "Off the Newsstands," advertisements for intriguing new or offbeat publications, with a chance to order sample copies.

The Writer. 120 Boylston St., Boston, MA 02116. Monthly.

Articles on a variety of kinds of writing, and market listings. Its most useful feature: a monthly list of prize offers, with details.

Writer's Digest. 1507 Dana Ave., Cincinnati, OH 45207. Monthly.

Every serious freelancer, whether beginner or pro, can profit from its market listings, writing and selling advice and money-making tips. Subscribe!

Writer's Journal. Box 65798, St. Paul, MN 55165. Monthly.

Formerly called *The Inkling Journal.* An attractive, wide-ranging magazine for writers at any level, with book reviews, a theme (e.g., sci-fi, article writing, self-publishing) for each issue and legal, poetry and inspirational columnists.

On Selling and Publishing

Appelbaum, Judith, and Nancy Evans, *How to Get Happily Published: A Complete and Candid Guide.* New York: Plume Books, 1982.

Accurately subtitled. Geared mainly to book writers but covers all aspects of writing, from getting ideas to contacting editors, from self-publishing to publicizing your work, from getting grants to learning to appreciate your success. Includes very comprehensive resource list.

Biagi, Shirley, *How to Write and Sell Magazine Articles.* Englewood Cliffs, NJ: Prentice-Hall, 1981.

This slim paperback includes especially good sections on how to slant an article idea, how to interview, how to take photos that you might be able to sell along with a manuscript and how to structure an article. Her sample query letters are more professional in tone than Burgett's.

Burgett, Gordon, *Query Letters/Cover Letters: How They Sell Your Writing.* P.O. Box 1001, Carpinteria, CA 93013: Communication Unlimited, 1985.

You may not want to emulate the casual, sometimes flippant tone of this apparently successful writer (he claims more than 900 publications), but his generally helpful advice and examples cover almost every possible situation for which some sort of query letter or cover letter is appropriate.

Burgett, Gordon, *How to Sell 75 Percent of Your Freelance Writing.* P.O. Box 1001, Carpinteria, CA 93013: Communication Unlimited, 1984.

Not as well produced and streamlined as *Query Letters/Cover Letters,* this pushes the most easily salable kinds of articles: nonfiction queried submissions and nonfiction simultaneous submissions. Format is confusing; running text is on right-hand pages, odds and ends on the left.

Cassill, Kay, *The Complete Handbook for Freelance Writers.* Cincinnati, OH: Writer's Digest Books, 1981.

Virtually everything you need to know about freelancing as a business, including how to scout opportunities, stay motivated, get into the black, promote yourself, plan for your future and keep necessary records. Includes glossary and good resource list.

Cool, Lisa Collier, *How to Sell Every Magazine Article You Write.* Cincinnati, OH: Writer's Digest Books, 1986.

An outstanding introduction to writing for magazines. In addition to thorough, sensible advice on freelancing basics, offers excellent advice on research, efficient writing, libel and copyright law, the inner workings of *Cosmo* and *Penthouse,* and an article makeover.

Cool, Lisa Collier, *How to Write Irresistible Query Letters.* Cincinnati, OH: Writer's Digest Books, 1987.

Superbly specific and sensible treatise on approaching editors, agents and publishers with query letters. Its highlight: twenty varied, convincing examples written by Cool and her students. Omits advice, however, on how to fine-tune queries for specific markets or how to follow through once your query has won you a go-ahead.

Duncan, Lois, *How to Write and Sell Your Personal Experiences,* 2nd ed. Cincinnati, OH: Writer's Digest Books, 1986.

Warm, absorbing, sometimes hilarious account of the opportunities, requirements and pitfalls of writing about things that happened (or almost or might have happened) to you. Very highly recommended.

Emerson, Connie, *Write on Target.* Cincinnati, OH: Writer's Digest Books, 1981.

Explains in obsessive, at times intriguing detail how to ape a magazine's approach and style by analyzing it down to the average sentence length, quotes per 500 words, polysyllabic words per hundred, types of titles and so on. If you're determined to break into a specific magazine, it might be worth trying Emerson's method.

Hanson, Nancy Edmonds, *How You Can Make $25,000 a Year Writing (No Matter Where You Live)*. Cincinnati, OH: Writer's Digest Books, 1987.

Explains how to succeed as a writer in the boonies, mainly by developing sidelines like PR, corporate and ghost writing, consulting, editing and photography. Valuable advice on setting your fees and scouting out or creating the hidden, lucrative opportunities where you live.

Kubis, Pat, and Bob Howland, *Writing Fiction, Nonfiction, and How to Publish*. Reston, VA: Reston Publishing Co., 1985.

Except for the authors' own unimpressive illustrative paragraphs, a very well done guide that is both wide-ranging and detailed. Somewhat expensive, but worth the investment if you are interested in writing fiction as well as nonfiction.

Peterson, Franklynn, and Judi Kesselman-Turkel, *The Magazine Writer's Handbook*. New York: Dodd, Mead & Co., 1987.

If you can only buy one book on this list, choose this one; you'll refer to it for a long time. Some of the more unusual topics covered: kinds of publications, ten basic article formats (with examples), how to use anecdotes and quotes, how and why to separate fact and opinion, how to deal with editors. Reprints the American Society of Journalists and Authors Code of Ethics, real query letters and assignment letters and more.

Poynter, Dan, and Mindy Bingham, *Is There a Book Inside You?* Santa Barbara, CA: Para Publishing, 1985.

Superbly conceived, well organized, nicely produced and uniquely slanted. Assumes that if you do indeed have a book inside you, you needn't actually write it yourself. Numerous self-rating questionnaires help you determine the publishing path (commercial, vanity, book producer, self-publishing or collaboration) that is right for you and your topic. Numerous checklists and sample sales copy; extensive resource list.

Raskin, Julie, and Carolyn Males, *How to Write and Sell a Column*. Cincinnati, OH: Writer's Digest Books, 1987.

Methodical advice for aspiring columnists, especially on how to define your purpose, audience and format and how to market or syndicate your column locally or nationally. Includes both failure and success stories.

West, Celeste, *Words in Our Pockets: The Feminist Writers Guild Handbook on How to Gain Power, Get Published and Get Paid.* Paradise, CA: Dustbooks, 1985.

Refreshingly frank and personal, humorous and enlightening. Experiences and advice concerning every aspect of working with words, from writing a book proposal to starting a writers' support group, from "establishment publishing" to doing it yourself. The forty-four contributors are women, mainly from the West Coast, who are passionate about communicating with integrity for appropriate rewards, including money and self-respect.

Zobel, Louise Purwin, *The Travel Writer's Handbook.* Cincinnati, OH: Writer's Digest Books, 1980.

Very highly recommended even if you hate to travel. Excellent chapters on studying the marketplace, pre-selling your stories and taking photos to submit with articles; includes a fascinating appendix on twelve kinds of (travel) articles.

On Style and Editing

Barzun, Jacques, *Simple and Direct: A Rhetoric for Writers.* New York: Harper & Row, 1976.

How to achieve clear, unobstructed written communication. As timeless as Strunk and White, explained in more depth. Distinctive chapter on tone, and twenty general principles of writing and revision (15: "Make fewer words do more work by proper balance, matching parts and tight construction").

Boston, Bruce O., *Stet! Tricks of the Trade for Writers and Editors.* Alexandria, VA: Editorial Experts, Inc., 1986.

For writers, this collection of short pieces from the newsletter of Editorial Experts, Inc., will be valuable for pointers on quotation tampering, grammar hotlines, cadences, when to use the passive voice, the top fifty misspelled words, how to check the quality of an index and much, much more.

Cheney, Theodore A. Rees, *Getting the Words Right: How to Revise, Edit & Rewrite.* Cincinnati, OH: Writer's Digest Books, 1983.

How to be your own editor. Interestingly written and packed with specific advice and examples. Worth buying, reading and rereading.

Cheney, Theodore A. Rees, *Writing Creative Nonfiction.* Cincinnati, OH: Writer's Digest Books, 1987.

More of a well-organized anthology of techniques Wolfe, Talese, Didion and company have made popular than instruction in writing literary nonfiction. Commentary is sometimes weak or unclear; lack of a bibliography further handicaps the book.

Chicago Manual of Style, 13th ed. Chicago: University of Chicago Press, 1982.

If you're serious about publishing, you should own a copy of this, the standard reference on punctuation, spelling, capitalization, treatment of numbers, documentation and indexing. Most magazines, newspapers and book publishers will edit your manuscript to conform with these or similar conventions; it helps to anticipate these changes.

Cook, Claire Kehrwald, *The MLA's Line by Line.* Boston: Houghton Mifflin, 1985.

Less lively and inspirational than Cheney's *Getting the Words Right.* Focus on improving sentences. Helpful for verbose writers or those unsure about proper punctuation.

Elbow, Peter, *Writing with Power.* New York: Oxford University Press, 1980.

Provides a panoply of useful techniques for coming up with ideas, getting feedback from readers and then selecting from and shaping your raw material. His last section circles round and round the mysterious phenomenon of voice in writing.

Franklin, Jon, *Writing for Story: Craft Secrets of Dramatic Nonfiction by a Two-time Pulitzer Prize Winner.* New York: New American Library, 1986.

If you've got a true story to tell, Franklin shows how to define the essence of your tale and make it dramatic and artful. Any writer could study his annotated prizewinning feature articles with great profit.

Gunther, Max, *Writing the Modern Magazine Article,* 4th ed. Boston: The Writer, Inc., 1982.

Thorough, readable introduction to writing for magazines. Worth consulting for its advice on writing article leads, transitions and endings and for its annotated texts of three quite long but lively, research-packed articles for *Travel & Leisure, Playboy* and *TV Guide* in, respectively, 1975, 1967 and 1972.

Miller, Casey, and Kate Swift, *The Handbook of Nonsexist Writing: For Writers, Editors & Speakers.* New York: Harper & Row, 1980.

Explains how and why to avoid sexual stereotypes, the pseudo-generic "he" and awkward "his/her" alternatives. Some editors and many potential readers agree that this is essential.

Murray, Donald M., *Read to Write: A Writing Process Reader*. New York: Holt, Rinehart & Winston, 1986.

Designed for college composition courses, but a treasure for serious writers. Besides three especially helpful case studies—including first drafts, final drafts and afterwords—by the writers of a software manual, personal-experience piece and science article, Murray includes his own astute, appreciative comments on all the selections.

O'Neill, Carol L., and Avima Ruder, *The Complete Guide to Editorial Freelancing*. New York: Barnes & Noble, 1979.

Sections on symbols and procedures of copy editing and proofreading, with detailed examples.

Pinckert, Robert C., *Pinckert's Practical Grammar: A Lively, Unintimidating Guide to Usage, Punctuation and Style*. Cincinnati, OH: Writer's Digest Books, 1986.

An iconoclastic work that could be extremely irritating to someone who cares about language. His attitude: when in Rome, write like the Romans, and if your dictionary says you're wrong, find another dictionary. ("Mistakes are only mistakes if they produce unintended results.") On the other hand, contains an illuminating, sensitive chapter on punctuating by sound and good advice on choosing words and developing appropriate style.

Queneau, Raymond, *Exercises in Style,* translated by Barbara Wright. New York: New Directions, 1981.

This extraordinary book presents one short scene in ninety-nine different styles, some outrageously inventive. If you feel your style has gotten boring, or just to have some fun, have a look.

Read, Herbert, *English Prose Style*. New York: Pantheon Books, 1980.

Originally published in 1928 and still valuable for its insight into the "soul" of English words, sentences and paragraphs.

Rodale, J. I., *The Synonym Finder*. New York: Warner Books, 1986.

Much richer and more contemporary than any *Roget's*. More than one million words and phrases, well organized in alphabetical format.

Strunk, William, Jr., and E. B. White, *The Elements of Style*, 3rd ed. New York: Macmillan, 1979.

Classic guide to clear, unpretentious writing.

Tarshis, Barry, *How to Write Like a Pro*. New York: New American Library, 1982.

This book's high points: fresh advice on "staging"—organizing information so that it's more easily digested by the reader—balancing factual and impressionistic details in skillful descriptions and orchestrating dialogue. Strongly recommended for writers who want to break into top markets.

Venolia, Jan, *Rewrite Right! How to Revise Your Way to Better Writing*. Berkeley: Ten Speed Press, 1987.

Very serviceable handbook on editing your own or another's writing. Includes rules of style, grammar, punctuation, word choice, spelling and layout and chapters on improving content, eliminating biases like sexism and racism and knowing how word processors, spell-checkers and grammar checkers can and can't help you.

Zinsser, William, *On Writing Well: An Informal Guide to Writing Nonfiction*, 3rd ed. New York: Harper & Row, 1985.

Twenty-two mainly amiable chapters on good writing by a great craftsman of clean, alert prose. Especially good on unity, science writing, the responsibilities of a critic or reviewer and the dehumanizing consequences of poor style.

The Inner Writer

Atchity, Kenneth, *A Writer's Time: A Guide to the Creative Process, from Vision Through Revision*. New York: Norton, 1986.

How to harness discipline to inspiration and bring ideas from vision to execution. Applies time-management theories to the writing process with obsessively detailed schedules and methods that may not work at all for some writers. Advice on arranging your office, plotting a book and publishing. Worthwhile for the chronically disorganized; Fritz (below) is clearer on the creative process.

Block, Lawrence, *Write for Your Life: The Book About the Seminar*. 3750 Estero Blvd., Fort Myers Beach, FL 33931: Write for Your Life, 1986.

Not as profound as Fritz's book (below), *Write for Your Life* applies power-of-positive-thinking ideas specifically to writing. Can help you identify the "personal laws" that hold you back from writing success.

Fritz, Robert, *The Path of Least Resistance: Principles for Creating What You Want to Create.* 9 Pickering Way, Salem, MA 01970: DMA, Inc., 1984.

The most concrete, helpful analysis that I've ever read of how to reach your creative goal and of strategies and habits that may be holding you back, by a composer who studied the creative process. Not a throw-away self-help book but hard-won wisdom on how to bring a vision to realization.

Goldberg, Natalie, *Writing Down the Bones.* Boston: Shambhala, 1986.

A personal application of Zen to writing. Because Goldberg favors honing inspiration, and excluding critical thinking, her anecdotal advice and considerable wisdom is likely to be more helpful to poets and such than to writers of nonfiction articles.

Klauser, Henriette Anne, *Writing on Both Sides of the Brain: Breakthrough Techniques for People Who Write.* New York: Harper & Row, 1986.

Designed to take the fear, trembling and procrastination out of writing by showing how to balance "right-brain" techniques like rapid writing and visualization with "left-brain" critical editing. If writing comes easily to you, however, you'll gain more from Rico's *Writing the Natural Way* (below). Klauser includes an excellent chapter on revision and a fascinating appendix on a "right-brain" method to improve your spelling.

Rico, Gabriele Lusser, *Writing the Natural Way.* Los Angeles: J. P. Tarcher, 1983.

The grandmother text of "right-brain" (intuitive) writing techniques. How to awaken and use your nonrational creative powers, with theory, examples and exercises. Interesting and helpful whether you're a fluent writer or blocked.

Rosenbaum, Jean, and Veryl Rosenbaum, *The Writer's Survival Guide: How to Cope with Rejection, Success, and 99 Other Hang-ups of the Writing Life.* Cincinnati OH: Writer's Digest Books, 1982.

From a psychiatrist and a psychoanalyst, a guide to escaping common and uncommon pitfalls that lie in wait for writers, and how to build up self-knowledge for a more productive lifestyle. Lots of fascinating, fresh examples. Especially good suggestions on constructing your personal psychohistory, avoiding transference with your editor and handling TV and radio talk shows (we should all be so lucky!).

Ueland, Brenda, *If You Want to Write: A Book About Art, Independence and Spirit.* St. Paul, MN: Graywolf Press, 1987.

Stresses the intrinsic rewards of tapping your creative power and the necessity for truthfulness and integrity, not speed, snappiness and efficiency, in art. Written in 1938 and still wonderfully persuasive and inspiring.

Writing and the Law

Bunnin, Brad, and Peter Beren, *Author Law & Strategies: A Legal Guide for the Working Writer*. Berkeley, CA: Nolo Press, 1983.

Excellent on the rights, responsibilities and options of book authors and publishers. Frank, clear discussion of libel, invasion of privacy, copyright, agents, collaboration and contracts. Many bonuses, including how to choose and use a literary lawyer and what counts as a contract. Neglects magazine writing except for one weak chapter.

Copyright Basics. Register of Copyrights, Library of Congress, Washington, DC 20559.

Basic overview of copyright regulations. Free. You can order this ("Circular R1") or blank registration forms (ask for "Form TX") by calling 202-287-9100 and leaving a message.

DuBoff, Leonard D., *The Law (in Plain English) for Writers*. Seattle: Madrona Publishers, 1987.

Much more depth on copyright, obscenity, writers' wills, partnerships (including unintended ones), agents' legal duties and kinds of libel than other sources. Includes careful, readable explanations of important legal concepts and significant U.S. cases. The author's recital of the broad range of bizarre suits writers have been dragged into is enough to make you pray, even if you haven't for years.

Henderson, Bruce, *How to Bulletproof Your Manuscript*. Cincinnati, OH: Writer's Digest Books, 1986.

How writers can avoid lawsuits. How to identify risky topics, check your facts, write up your material scrupulously and deal with trouble when it does arise. Invaluable for investigative reporters, writers of fact-based fiction and others who do or should worry about accusations of libel.

Tax Guide for College Teachers. P.O. Box 1718, College Park, MD 20740: Academic Information Service. Annually updated.

Although designed for college teachers, contains the most detailed and reliable advice available on deducting expenses of writing and research from your taxes for anyone who writes.

Tax Guide for Small Businesses. Internal Revenue Service, Washington, DC 20224.

Free, annually updated. You can obtain this or other IRS publications by calling 1-800-424-FORM.

Miscellaneous

Abrams, Lawrence F., *Photography for Writers.* P.O. Box 268, Washau, WI 54402: Entwood Publishing, 1986.

A crisply written guide that could help turn you from a writer into a writer-photographer. Comprehensive how-to-photograph information slanted specifically for submitting photos with articles. Abrams also includes results of a survey of editors' photo preferences and fourteen pages of what's-wrong-with-this-photo to test your mastery of good photo technique.

Biagi, Shirley, *Interviews That Work: A Practical Guide for Journalists.* Belmont, CA: Wadsworth, 1986.

Though written for aspiring newspaper and broadcast reporters, this text includes three chapters—on how to ask good questions, whether to use direct quotes or paraphrase, and how to quote sources in articles—that can help a freelancer get and use the material that will spice up her work.

Grants and Awards Available to American Writers. 568 Broadway, New York, NY 10012: PEN American Center.

Comprehensive, updated biannually. Includes listings for writers' colonies.

National Writers Union, 13 Astor Place, 7th Floor, New York, NY 10003, (212) 254-0279.

Organization that represents the interests of all writers. Within the past several years, has negotiated standard contracts and improved pay with several magazines. In addition to a newsletter, health insurance and discounts on certain books, computers and car rentals, members have access to advice on contracts and (sometimes spectacularly expeditious) handling of grievances against publishers. Dues vary depending on how much money you make from your writing.

Index

ABOUT THE AUTHOR

Since receiving her Ph.D. in philosophy from Cornell University in 1978, Marcia Yudkin has taught philosophy at Smith College, worked as a freelance writer and editor and taught writing at Boston University, Babson College and the University of Massachusetts. Her publications include fiction in *Yankee, Feldspar Prize Stories* and *Art Times* and nonfiction in the *New York Times, Boston Globe, Ms., Psychology Today, The Progressive,* the *Village Voice* and others. In 1983–84 she was a writer and editor for the Foreign Languages Press in Beijing, China. In 1986 two books of hers appeared: *Making Good: Private Business in Socialist China* (Foreign Languages Press) and (with Janice Moulton) *Guidebook for Publishing Philosophy* (American Philosophical Association). She lives in Boston.